The Secrets to Restaurant Management and Staff Training

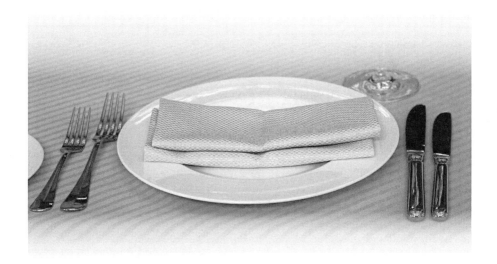

The Missing Pieces
to a Highly Successful
Restaurant Operation

by Christine J. Lueders

The Secrets to Restaurant Management and Staff Training:
The Missing Pieces to a Highly Successful Restaurant Operation

Library of Congress Cataloging-in-Publication Data

Names: Lueders, Christine J., author.
Title: The secrets to restaurant management and staff training : the missing
   pieces to a highly successful restaurant operation / by Christine J.
   Lueders.
Description: Ocala, Florida : Atlantic Publishing Group, Inc., 2017. |
   Includes bibliographical references and index.
Identifiers: LCCN 2017022601 (print) | LCCN 2017023672 (ebook) | ISBN
   9781620234129 (ebook) | ISBN 9781620234112 (alk. paper) | ISBN 1620234114 (alk.
   paper) | ISBN 9781620234129 (E-book)
Subjects: LCSH: Restaurant management. | Restaurants--Personnel management.
Classification: LCC TX911.3.M27 (ebook) | LCC TX911.3.M27 L84 2017 (print) |
   DDC 647.95068--dc23
LC record available at https://lccn.loc.gov/2017022601

Printed in the United States

PROJECT MANAGER AND EDITOR: Lisa McGinnes • lisa@lisamcginnes.com
COVER & JACKET DESIGN: Nicole Sturk • nicolejonessturk@gmail.com
INTERIOR LAYOUT: Antoinette D'Amore • addesign@videotron.ca

Over the years, we have adopted a number of dogs from rescues and shelters. First there was Bear and after he passed, Ginger and Scout. Now, we have Kira, another rescue. They have brought immense joy and love not just into our lives, but into the lives of all who met them.

We want you to know a portion of the profits of this book will be donated in Bear, Ginger and Scout's memory to local animal shelters, parks, conservation organizations, and other individuals and nonprofit organizations in need of assistance.

– Douglas & Sherri Brown,
President & Vice-President of Atlantic Publishing

Thank you

*M*any of my ideas for this book were written while I was working as a manager or waitress over the past five years. As you may imagine all of my notes were on small pieces of paper. So, I would like to thank my mom, Ruth Lueders, for taking all of my slips of paper, trying to make sense out of my scribbles (not understanding restaurant terminology), and entering everything into the computer. During this process we had our share of misunderstandings and eye-opening discussions, but at the same time a whole lot of fun! She believed in me, supported me, and encouraged me all the way!

Thank you to the Newicks family, who own a seafood restaurant in New Hampshire, for giving me my first opportunity to become a manager and trainer. The knowledge I gained over the years gave me the understanding of how important a good manager is to the culture of a restaurant and the importance of a good relationship between managers and the staff.

Thank you Mr. Michael Besson, a general manager where I currently work, for taking an interest in reading my manuscript and giving me his personal views and encouragement.

I would also like to thank Mr. Brown, owner of Atlantic Publishing, for understanding the significance this book may have on the restaurant industry, and my editors Lisa McGinnes and Rebekah Slonim for their understanding, suggestions, and patience in answering all my questions.

Table of Contents

Introduction

When managers take care of the staff, the staff will take care of the guests, and the guests will always come back.

The hospitality industry is one of the fastest growing industries, and it incorporates many diverse areas with multiple jobs requiring multiple skills.

For those who work in the restaurant industry, the term hospitality means "the quality or disposition of receiving and treating people in a warm, friendly, and generous way." This kind of behavior should be applied not only to guests but also to employees. We all know that we should treat our guests this way, but we neglect to treat the people who actually do the job — our co-workers — this way.

The purpose of this book is not to teach the techniques needed for the jobs or the physical aspects, but to show everyone connected to a restaurant operation — owners, managers, and staff — how understanding individual actions, work relationships, and personal feelings can lead to mutual respect and unity which in turn can decrease problems between managers, staff, and guests; decrease turnover rates due to job dissatisfaction; and at the same time increase profits for staff and the establishment through increased guest satisfaction.

For staff members, there are many books written to help them perform their jobs better and universities that cater to culinary arts degrees. For owners and managers, there are books on how to set-up and start a restaurant, how to run a restaurant, and there are articles about the requirements for becoming a great manager or leader.

This book is focused on three main areas:

1. **Respect**

    In order to decrease turnover rates and problems associated with staff and guests, people working in an establishment need to earn and show respect for each other. Since most of the staff is under 30 years of age, some managers tend to believe that these young adults don't know any better, that they do what they want, or that they don't follow orders. On the other hand, staff members feel that they aren't being taken seriously, that they are not being heard, or that the managers just don't care.

    Respect is earned — not given — no matter what position a person holds, and this respect is earned — or lost — through actions.

2. **Proper Training**

Managers uphold rules, policies, and procedures, but they should also teach staff the proper ways of doing the job while maintaining respect and a receptive ear in order to create a positive atmosphere. They should see themselves as teachers or coaches building understanding, respect, and unity.

3. **Delegating and following through**

Companies can stress the importance of their mission and vision statements; they can write them down in handbooks, talk about them, or even post them on bulletin boards, but unless they are enforced through actions and words, no one will follow them or even care to follow them.

When a manager tells the staff that he or she intends to do something or fix a problem, he or she has to follow through on it. **Actions will speak louder than words** — for staff and managers.

The majority of this book will focus on the actions of hosts, servers, and managers, but will also touch on bartenders and take-out service. This book does not spend time on cocktail waitresses, bussers, barbacks (or bartender's assistant), or food runners. Most places don't have these positions because they are normally a part of the servers' or bartenders' roles.

This book will guide individual managers and staff to possible solutions on how to improve the state of their work environment, and shows the reasoning behind suggested actions. It draws on over 30 years of my own experience with different working techniques as well as some tricks of the trade that I have established over the years. The book will provide suggestions on how to perform certain tasks not taught in other books and training programs, and also some specific skills such as how to handle inventory, interior setups, and much more. The book is a guideline to help make jobs easier, not an industry-standard practice.

When going through this book, it is important to start reading at the beginning to understand each position. I highly recommend that owners and managers read the entire book due to the fact that I describe possible ways of enhancing workflow, not only in manager sections, but also in sections for staff members. This book is set up to help personnel excel in every position **starting with the lowest and continuing through every level** as more knowledge and understanding is required. Each section will give guidelines, reasons for those guidelines, and examples to help management and staff members develop a better understanding and achieve a higher performance.

Keep in mind that this book contains restaurant terminology that may seem foreign to those unfamiliar with the lingo. For example, a server might say, "I'm going to run the food on the floor to the tables." What he or she means is, "I'm going to serve the food in the restaurant to the guests." If you already work in hospitality, you may be very familiar with all of these terms, but to those who might be confused, we have included sidebars that explain the lingo.

Part One of the book covers general suggestions that **all** employees will benefit from. Part Two covers hosting; Part Three covers serving, take-out service, and bartending; and Part Four covers management. The appendix has examples of training programs, teamwork, lists of interview questions, test questions, terminologies, some general information such as job boards and online support, and much more.

My hope is that these suggestions and techniques will help to create a happier work environment, a smoother service, and ultimately, a more profitable restaurant.

Part One

All Staff Members

Chapter 1

General Information

> *"You never get a second chance*
> *to make a good first impression."*
>
> ~ *Will Rogers*

Presentation

How many times have you heard that quote? Probably some version of it many times.

Here's a new take on it: "Every time you walk into the dining room, think of yourself as being on stage in front of an audience." You're making a first impression — and your performance is being watched.

Both of these quotes express powerful ideas, but ask yourself if you really understand them, and, if you do, how your actions demonstrate your understanding.

I know that some of my first impressions could have been a whole lot better in my early years in the restaurant business. As for being on stage, let's just say I made my share of mistakes. I thought my nose was wet, so I just wiped it. I am sure that I yawned a couple of times without putting my hand in front of my mouth, and I was caught chewing gum — an especially bad first impression for a server. I really did forget to spit it out before I went to the table.

It's hard sometimes to remember all of the details, but the key is to be aware of things you are doing in the dining room. So, in keeping with the term of hospitality, if you are in view of a guest, my best advice would be to smile all the time — no matter what the situation might be — and say "Sorry" (and mean it) when you mess up.

The more guests feel that they are welcome and believe that you want them to enjoy the food, the atmosphere, and generally have a good time, the more they will feel that they can trust you. Any problems you may have, either inside or outside the workplace, should not show on your face, especially when things go wrong. I know that this is easier said than done, but as an employee, and for the success of the company, you have to try.

Remember: your world is a stage, so be careful with what you do in it.

Attitude

"Don't have one, unless it's a good one."

They say that "negative talk breeds negative actions," and that is so true! Negative talk brings the morale down and tends to spread anger. When people are constantly complaining or talking negatively about others, it's hard for anyone to feel positive. There will always be problems no matter where you work or what you do. Problems are unavoidable, and whether they are work problems or personal problems is irrelevant. How you present yourself in a bad situation is what will matter. Your attitude will transcend to your guests and co-workers. They will get the vibes you are sending them, and their impressions will reflect on you and the restaurant.

It is also said that "a happy, upbeat person is infectious." Which person do you think would make more money — the one with a sour expression on his or her face or the one seeming cheerful and happy? I know, this is one of those "Duh" questions, but think about the times when you didn't make as much money as on other days. What were you thinking about?

Even though you may have to deal with certain problem guests, which can be very trying for everyone who has direct contact with them, you still have to be pleasant. When working in the field of hospitality, you must be able to put your personal feelings aside.

A good attitude is not something you should try to achieve completely on your own. If you can't fix your problems yourself, talk to a person who can help you. It would be awesome if this person were your boss. This goes for managers, too, if you have a general or regional manager. Being able to go to this person and have him or her listen and understand could help lift your spirits.

For instance, it might be helpful for a server to talk to his or her boss or confidante about this problem: Giving out coupons, reward cards, and so on to attract guests is a big issue in the restaurant business. Those promotional tools attract some people who just come in to get something for nothing instead of rewarding the patrons who like the restaurant, the food, and the service. Having to serve those "opportunists" with the customary smiles and friendliness is very frustrating for a server when he or she knows that those guests are also too cheap to leave a proper tip. Understanding why they do this kind of marketing does not change this situation, but it may make it easier to be pleasant if you know that someone sympathizes with the difficulty.

Here is an example for hosts: Hosts deal with people who do not want to sit where the hosts lead them. That's an understatement, is it not? They want to pick their own tables, even if it is in a section that is closed, or at a table that is dirty. Doesn't that happen all the time? So, in these situations, always have a smile on your face and have a grin-and-bear-it attitude.

Atmosphere

Be careful with background music! It is common knowledge that, when the music is slow, people tend to eat slower and take their time. It is the opposite when playing fast music. The owner or manager must decide which speed to choose and for what time of the day.

For instance: A manager might want to play faster music from 5 to 8 p.m. to get people in and out faster, but slower music from 2 to 5 p.m. to allow the parking lot to fill up during the off times, giving an illusion that the restaurant is always busy. It is fun to test and interesting to watch. The background music is something for the managers to deal with, but the other staff members may want to be aware of this.

Cleanliness and hygiene

OK, here we go. There are some things you may not know, so don't skip over this section just yet.

1. **Perfume and Cologne:** Make sure they are subtle and not too overpowering. A guest wants to smell the food, not your fragrance. If in doubt, always ask another server for feedback.

2. **Jewelry:** If you are wearing jewelry, keep it simple, and wear only one or two pieces of the same type at a time. Diamonds (except an engagement ring) and precious stones should be avoided even if they are not real. If you wear a lot of jewelry, or it looks expensive, your guests will presume that you have excess money to spend on jewelry and may not tip as well no matter how good your service is. Earrings should not be bigger than a quarter and should not be dangling. Large earrings look unprofessional and pose a health hazard if they get caught on a tray and are accidentally ripped off. Some places limit rings to just a wedding ring and an engagement ring because they fear that if food is trapped under the band, it can form bacteria when hands are not washed carefully.

3. **Hair:** OK, here is another one of those "No Duh" sentences: No one wants to find a hair in his or her food. So, make sure that your hair is cut properly, tied securely, braided, or, for women, placed in a bun, and that no spikes are sticking out. I know this is hard when having to cope with humidity, but gel or mousse really comes in handy. Make sure your hair does not touch the food when you are carrying a tray on your shoulder. It can happen if you have a swinging ponytail or braid.

4. **Nails:** Nails should be short, trimmed, and clean at all times. This is often overlooked, but when a guest sees dirt under your nails, he or she is immediately turned off. You should also omit nail polish. Nail polish has the tendency to chip, peel, or melt under heat lamps, and particles may fall on the food or elsewhere. Let's face it — if this happens, it really does not look good either.

5. **Makeup:** Try to make it look natural and in good taste. This will show that you are a professional in your field.

Society is resisting trends, and when guests see pink or other bright-colored hair, black nails, or exotic makeup, they get distracted and do not realize how great the service is. I know, you're on stage, but be tasteful.

Uniforms

No matter what your uniform consists of, your attire should always be neat and clean. If you are wearing a white shirt, your undershirt should also be white so it does not shine through. You would not believe how many employees decide to wear black bras or t-shirts under a white shirt. It just looks tacky and unprofessional. The shirts should be without wrinkles or stains, and they should be tucked in. Aprons should also be clean. Remember: your apron is at eye level with the guests.

Pants should not be too short or too long so that they can be stepped on; they should also not be worn through. The size should be appropriate (meaning that they are not too baggy or too tight). They also should be free from spills and food particles. If something gets spilled on them during the shift, make sure you clean them up right away to the best of your ability. Use soda water and/or a Tide® to Go Instant Stain Remover. A final detail — shoes should not have holes in them, they should be slip resistant, and they should be clean! Yes, guests look at those, too.

Cleanliness throughout the restaurant

This is not an easy task, but with everyone on the same page, it becomes second nature to pick things up off the floor or clean something.

For Servers:
(Also check Part Three: Servers)

1. Are tables, chairs, or benches clean? I have found lots of coins while cleaning booths. Every penny counts.

2. What about the floor, salt and pepper shakers, or sugar caddies? I once found a phone on the floor and wondered how long it had been there since it was in vibrate mode.

3. What about the silverware? Does it have spots or food particles on it? I always came in early just to polish the knives.

4. What about the bread plates? Do they have any butter wrappers stuck to the bottom of them?

5. Is there dust on the light fixtures or on any trim? Yes, people notice these things.

For Hosts:
(Also check Part Two: Hosts)

1. Is the host stand cleaned and organized?

2. Are the waiting area chairs or benches — and surrounding areas — clean?

3. Are the menus clean and not torn? I once opened a menu and found gum. Good thing it was I who found it and not a guest!

4. Are the windows and doors clean from fingerprints? I know that those small handprints look cute, but …

5. Is there any dust? Again, guests will notice.

For Everyone, including Managers:
(Also check Part Four: Managers)

1. Are the kitchen floors clean? (If a guest can see them, they had better be clean.)

2. And the most important part: Are the restrooms clean? If they are not, everyone should help here. It is said that "if the restrooms are clean, then so is everything else in the restaurant."

One thing I must mention because it happens way too often is that restaurant employees often leave the table they used during their break without cleaning up after themselves. Everybody should make sure that the table is clean and reset with silverware, napkins, or whatever else is needed for seating the next guests. This is a courtesy and shows respect for your co-workers.

Safety in the workplace

It still amazes me that, even today, staff members will walk right past a lemon wedge, a butter pat, or an ice cube on the floor without cleaning it up. Do people really not care for the safety of their co-workers, let alone the guests? Let's not make this the norm.

Let's make sure that, if there are any spills, leaks, or puddles, someone stays until it is cleaned and a "Wet Floor" sign is placed over the drying area, the floors are kept free of clutter and crowding, all the rugs and mats are in place and stay in place, broken glass has been swept up to avoid somebody getting injured, and cutting gloves and non-slip shoes are worn by everybody when needed.

Training

Because every position requires a large amount of training for an employee to become efficient, there will be training tips and guidelines in each category of this book. Things will come up that are not taught in classrooms — this book has information that will be hard to find anywhere else.

Yet, because this book of necessity cannot cover everything, knowing and understanding the way your company operates is essential to your achievements. After reading this book, you'll already have a good grasp on the most important thing that you'll learn in training — the main focus should always remain on guest satisfaction and interaction with the guests. If you're a teen about to start your very first job working at a restaurant, this should be a relief. If you focus on quality guest service, all the specifics and complexities of being a host or server will eventually fall into place.

Remember that when you go to training. We have all heard the term "sink or swim," and restaurants sometimes approach training that way. They have a tendency to train people and throw them into the job having minimal support. This action needs to be eliminated. Can you even imagine a smooth transition into a new restaurant job with that method? Unheard of, right?

So even if you're not lucky enough to get a manager and trainers who know to move slowly and how to help you work up to success, this book will give you a leg up — both with all the sometimes-neglected details of good service that it explains and by reminding you about what's most important in the restaurant industry.

Still, managers need to stop training by information overload.

If you're a manager, remember why many teens work in restaurants to begin with — and what they stand to learn from doing so. Many teenagers get their first job in a restaurant because often no experience is necessary. This experience itself is the most valuable part for a person at this age. It teaches not only a job, but also a work ethic, being a part of a team, communication and its importance, and, above all, how to deal with all sorts of people. You want to make it as easy as possible for your teenage employees and other new employees to learn these things.

Knowledge is the key to success. Nothing can replace good training and experience on the job. You've got to tell them what they need to know — and at a rate at which they can process it. And you should do so while tying everything back to the focal point — guest satisfaction.

You should also always consider that everyone is going to interact with guests in his or her own way.

Working in the restaurant industry is one of the most interactive professions, but all people are different in personality and actions, and every situation they will find themselves in is different. Training should factor in a worker's unique personality and help him or her figure out ways that he or she can respond to the varying situations of restaurant work. Don't try to make the new employee interact with guests in the same way you do.

Trainers should embrace these differences and always keep an open mind to making new friends or acquaintances both with co-workers and guests.

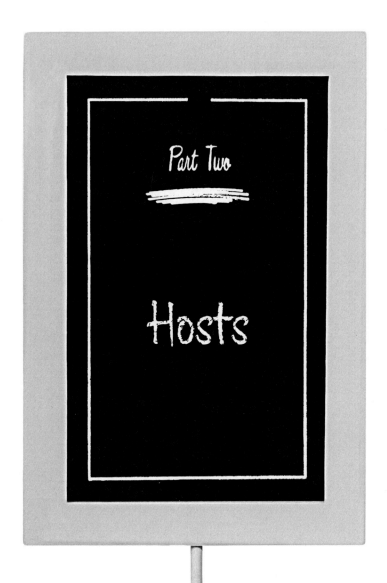

Part Two

Hosts

Chapter 2

General Information

Starting Off on the Right Foot

A host represents the establishment and is in control of the entire flow of a restaurant. He or she holds the most important position — a position that is critical to achieving a smoothly running operation on a daily basis, especially during the holiday season.

From the time guests come in, the host controls when they will be seated, and which servers will be taking care of them, and this, in turn, controls the pace at which orders will enter the kitchen. The host is also the last defense when it comes to preventing the guest from leaving unhappy!

With this kind of importance, all individuals should attain and maintain a high quality of professionalism. This can be achieved with proper training and job guidance. The establishment needs to understand this concept and set guidelines that are easy to understand. Some of those guidelines can be found throughout this section, are already written by the establishment, or can be a combination of both.

The position of "host" should be given only to people who are well-trained and understand the flow, principles, and concepts of the restaurant. Since many establishments are using different computer programs, most of their training involves those programs. I will not be talking about them, but will give only general knowledge and suggestions in this section.

Ninety percent of restaurants employ hosts who are not yet 18 years of age, because, under state regulations, people under 18 are not yet allowed to work as servers and serve alcoholic drinks. In some states, that age is 19 or 21. That being the case, the following information and suggestions are very detailed for the benefit of people who were not trained and have never had a host job before, and because a host has the biggest responsibility in a restaurant. Have I mentioned this already? If I repeat myself, it's because it's important!

Bathrooms

People will judge a restaurant by the cleanliness of the bathrooms. A messy bathroom can represent a messy restaurant — at least in a guest's eyes. If the condition of the bathrooms is part of your job requirements — like making sure that they are stocked with soap, toilet paper, and hand towels; that the trash is not overflowing; and that the floors are clean — you should check the bathrooms every hour when the restaurant is not busy, and every 15 minutes to half an hour when business increases. Both bathrooms should have a check-off list on the back of the door that should be initialed after each inspection. Multiple lists can be put into plastic sheet protectors and hung on the back of the door.

Example:

Date	Soap	Toilet Paper	Hand Towel	Floors	Trash	Init.

Keep items in stock

During the shift, if the last box of something (like crayons) is opened or the items are running low, you should refill the supplies. If the last of something is taken from the storage area, tell the managers so that they can order more.

Table orientation

One thing that is often overlooked is table orientation. Before opening the restaurant, stand in front of the dining room and look at all the tables to see that they are straightened and appealing to the eye. Alignment of the tables shows order and creates a visual appeal. If four-tops are not straight, or are not corner to corner, it may have a negative effect on guests. They may not know what makes them feel uncomfortable when asked, but their brain subconsciously knows that something is off.

A "four-top" is a square table that seats up to four guests.

No favoritism

Playing favorites should never be done — don't pick favorite servers and always give them the best or the most tables to serve. You are dealing with people's livelihoods! It can also be a morale disaster. The servers being favored will get the cold shoulder from the staff not being favored. When favoritism is practiced in an establishment, people will already be angry when they come in to work, will constantly complain, and the morale goes down from there. On the other hand, if everyone is treated equally, the staff will work together and pull for each other. Teamwork will help make money for everyone.

Management will know when someone is practicing favoritism. It shows on their daily reports. There may be certain consequences that may be listed in the Rules, Regulations, and Guidelines of the establishment.

Know your servers

You must know and understand the servers, what they can handle, their speed of service, and their personalities. You also have to be able to read the guests. For example, when there are children in the group, the servers have to give them more attention and be more patient. So, you might want a server who is good with kids. Many times, the host has to make a judgment call based on each situation, but knowing the servers can help with these decisions.

Make sure that servers are not overwhelmed and that the cooks have enough time to get the food out in a timely manner. This can only be achieved through proper timing and seating. Just because a table is available does not mean that it should be seated immediately.

Large groups

We all know that servers need to "flip tables" in order to earn money, because they do not normally receive minimum wage. The bulk of their income comes from tips. Therefore, a host should try to avoid seating a larger party until at least half of the party is present, but check the establishment's guidelines. Larger groups tend to make a reservation so they do not have to wait, but when only a few people are seated and the rest of the party does not arrive for another hour or so (yes, no exaggeration, I have seen this happen many times), it is not fair to the server or the other guests. Servers miss out on flipping tables, and other guests have to wait unnecessarily.

"Flipping tables" means serving guests quickly so that you can get as many tables as possible in as short of time as possible. This is how servers maximize the amount of money they make in a single shift.

If the restaurant's policy states that large parties cannot be seated until everyone has arrived, you can tell the guests about the policy when they complain and want to be seated right away, and the manager will back you up.

Communication

You will have to understand how important your position is and that "communication is the key to success." You must be in constant communication with the floor manager, the servers, the main host, and the kitchen staff.

The servers should be asked if they are OK with handling another party on top of the guests they already have to serve. This way, not only can the server relay any information to you, but it also helps to make sure the guests will be properly attended to. This creates understanding and respect.

You would want to seat a large party with a person who is known as a strong server, not with a new server or a server who would not be able to handle the party properly. Larger parties that require two servers can be served by a new server and a strong server.

With multiple hosts on duty (see Chapter 3) the second host should tell the main host if people do not sit where they are supposed to sit, what tables are available, which tables are dirty, which guests may be leaving soon, and any other important information.

The kitchen should be alerted when a large party is coming in even if they are not immediately seated but are waiting for other guests to arrive. When everybody is present, the kitchen should be told again that they will soon be ordering. This is where an "Open Menu Count" comes in handy. (See Chapter 4.)

An "Open Menu Count" consists of all of the menus that are on the tables in front of guests who have not ordered yet.

The manager should be alerted to any problems or potential problems, such as nearing the quoted wait time, a party not being on the wait-list at all, etc. This communication will ensure that the guests will get great service while also eliminating anxiety for everyone.

Chapter 3

Host Stand

Host stand

Before shifts start, make sure that you have everything you will need: regular menus, gluten-free menus, kids' menus, crayons, pens, markers, staples, etc. Some computers show wait-list sheets, server count sheets, server section maps, etc. — but if they are not on the computer, those items will also be needed.

The host stand should be clean, neat, organized, and presentable to entering guests, so make sure that it is always free of scattered menus or other papers and that the wastepaper baskets are emptied.

Guest questions

As a host, you will have to answer many questions while on the job. The more you know, the more professional you will be, and the better you will be serving the guests. Some of the questions that may be asked are: "What is the room capacity for large parties?"; "Do you have special menus for banquets, carry-outs, in Braille, for gluten-free guests, etc.?"; or "What are the specials for the day?" When asked where the restrooms are, you should not just point or give directions — you should take the person there personally, if possible.

Positioning

When two or more hosts are on duty at the same time, one of them should always be at the host stand. The host at the host stand would be the main host or the first host. The other hosts follow the instructions the main host gives them, including seating guests, putting tables together, rolling more silverware, etc.

If you are the only one on duty and have to leave for any length of time, have a manager or server fill in to greet the guests. If the guests cannot be seated for whatever reason, then the manager or server could just say, "The host will be right with you."

Floor plans

Make sure that the servers' names are entered in sections on the chart or on the computer before the restaurant opens — or before a shift change.

When making a floor plan, you or the manager should make sure that the servers are put into positions that are visible to the guests. If incoming guests think that the restaurant is filled up because they do not see an open table, it's easier for them to be willing to go on a wait. If the restaurant does not take reservations, and the incoming guests see an open table they may just say, "Why can't we sit there?" They will not care about any explanation that is given to them.

Greeting guests

Show professionalism when greeting guests by never using the terms "buddy," "fellows," "friends," or especially not "guys." Those terms can be offensive or inappropriate, and guests will start off with a bad experience. Endearments like "honey," "sweetie," etc. are also best avoided — they can sound saccharine and overly personal. The terms "ma'am," "sir," "ladies," and "gentlemen" are much better. Or you could just simply say, "Good morning (or afternoon or evening). Welcome to ____." Another good option: "Hello, welcome to ____. How many are in your party?" Acknowledging the new guests is a big deal. So, if you are busy and cannot properly greet them, just say, "I'll be right with you."

Don't say "Just one?"

Whenever I hear a host say "Just one?" to an incoming single guest, I wonder what the guest may be thinking. Does he or she think that the host is implying that he or she is lonely? A better question to ask would be: "How many are in your party?" It is always possible that more people will come in to join the single guest. When it turns out that the person is alone, the host can ask where he or she would like to eat — at the full-service bar, at a table, or in a booth. If the guest is looking for company, he or she may want to sit at the bar and talk to others, or if the guest wants to be by himself or herself, the guest will choose a table or a booth. Knowing this will help you to take your guest to the best place for him or her to eat.

Size of people/handicapped people

In order not to embarrass anyone, you must make some judgment calls when it comes to seating people. That means that you do not want to seat a guest in a booth he or she might not fit into comfortably. The same goes for the bar where the chairs might be too tall, and the person might have a problem getting up there. The best way is to ask the guest, "Would you like to sit at a table, a booth, or the bar?" If a guest asks for a table right when he or she walks in, an embarrassing moment probably happened to him or her before. If guests use crutches, walkers, or have any other obvious difficulties walking, try to seat them as close to the front door as possible. Not only is this considerate, but also it shows the guests that you care.

Answering the phone

Before answering the phone have a list in front of you showing the proper information: name of the restaurant, address, phone number, hours of operation, and, if the place is part of a chain, the names and addresses of others in the chain that are close by. The list should also show the name of the owner or manager on duty. And, of course, a menu should be handy so you can answer any food-related questions. If you do not know the answer, just state: "Sorry, I'm not sure, but if you will hold a moment, I will find out." One should never try to bluff or give the wrong information.

People call all the time for information, to make a reservation, or to order food for take-out. You should say, for instance: "Thank you for calling (restaurant name), my name is (name), how may I assist you?" You should not say, "How may I help you?" That implies that they need help when they may not. (OK, so some people may need help, but you cannot tell them that.)

Every word should always be said with a smile, because the caller can actually hear that smile through the phone. After saying the skit, listen very carefully to what is being said in return. If you do not hear clearly or do not quite understand, you should politely ask them to repeat: "I'm sorry, I didn't hear (or understand) what you said. Will you tell me again?" Then you should repeat what you thought the person may have said to make sure that there is no misunderstanding. This is especially important when it is very noisy in the restaurant, and/or you take a to-go order. (More about this in the to-go section.)

The skit is the prepared verbiage that you always say to guests in a given situation. For instance, as a host, your "skit" for greeting guests is, "Welcome! How many are in your party?"

Guests leaving

When guests are leaving the restaurant, always thank them for coming in, wish them a good night, and tell them to come back soon.

When the guests answer you, try to read their mood. Do they have smiles on their faces when they say "Thanks" happily, or do they speak in low tones and are anxious to leave, indicating that something went wrong? **You are the last person in the restaurant who can make things**

right before they walk out the door. Ask them if everything was OK and try to get more information if there was a problem. If they answer, then they want people to know. You can apologize to them and at the same time try to get a manager to come and help with the situation. If they just want to rush out the door and do not want to talk to a manager, try to give them the manager's business card and say something like: "Our manager would really like to hear from you. You can email or call him or her."

A restaurant never wants people to leave angry. As the saying goes: "When one person has a bad experience, he or she will tell 10 other people, and when the person has a good experience, he or she may only tell one person."

Chapter 4

Seating

Counting system

Try to be as fair as possible to the servers when seating guests. You would not want them to stand around with nothing to do, but neither would you want them running around trying to give service to all their guests at once, thereby leaving guests dissatisfied.

A way to avoid this situation is to count the people that need to be attended to and not to count tables that need to be serviced. When you only count tables, you are not taking into consideration how many people are actually sitting at each table. There could be two tables with only two people at each, equaling four people; or there could be one five-top and one eight-top, which would make a total of thirteen people one server has to take care of. The server may get overwhelmed, and the guests will be dissatisfied because they will not get the proper attention.

Instead, if you seat by the number of people in the party, you will have more equilibrium. Every server can earn money and is more relaxed. A staff that is calm and in control will give better service to the guests. You may have to fit parties wherever there may be room but always check with the server and try to do the counting system as much as you can.

Here is an example:

Name								
Sue	2/2	2/4	5/9	3/12	2/14	2/16	6/22	2/24
Matt	2/2	3/5	2/7	2/9	2/11	3/14	2/16	
Chris	4/4	2/6	2/8	4/12	1/13	2/15	4/19	

In the example, the first number is the number of guests in the party. The second number is the total number of guests the server has attended to. As it shows, Sue has more guests than the other two servers. In this case, the host would want to seat the server with the lowest guest count (Matt) with more guests, and then the server with the next lowest guest count (Chris), as shown in the example below.

For example:

Name									
Sue	2/2	2/4	5/9	3/12	2/14	2/16	6/22	2/24	
Matt	2/2	3/5	2/7	2/9	2/11	3/14	2/16	2/18	2/20	4/24

Name									
Chris	4/4	2/6	2/8	4/12	1/13	2/15	4/19	2/21	2/23	

Openers

When you come into work, there are already some servers called "openers" busy setting things up for the upcoming shift. These openers do a lot of work ahead of time before the doors are opened to the first guests and should be seated with the first two or three tables even though the other servers that came into work the shift are already present. This not only helps to keep up the morale, but also makes it worthwhile for a person to come in early to set things up. Otherwise nobody would want to be an opener.

"Openers" are servers who help prepare the restaurant before the doors open by setting things up. They should receive the first several tables once people are being seated.

If the establishment has servers scheduled for different times of the day, it is most important not to have them catch up with other servers who have been there longer.

You can mark a line going down on a graph for each hour a server is scheduled so that the tables for the openers are not counted when other servers report to work, and so servers who start at 11 a.m. do not catch up with servers who started at 10 a.m.

For example:

Time	Name	Tables		Reset		
10	Sue	2/2	2/4	3/3	1/4	?
10	Matt	2/2	3/5	2/2	2/4	?
11	Chris	X	X	2/2	?	?
11	Jess	X	X	4/4	?	?
noon	Nate	X	X	X	X	?

A question mark shows the name of the server next to be sat going from the top down. If people do not come in before 11 a.m. the same pattern should still be applied. It's fine if the server gets more tables to serve beforehand as long as the pattern is kept. When counting, you have to make sure that the openers' totals are reset. This reset happens every time a new server is placed on the floor.

When you are working at night, know which servers are working two shifts that day. Know who the closers are. Then you will know who to let go when business slows down once the manager tells you to cut.

Women

Here is something to keep in mind. When two or more women come in and are chatting up a storm saying that they have not seen one another for a long time, you may want to seat them with a server who will be working later than the others. Those ladies will probably sit and chat for a long time after they are done with their meals.

Requests

If guests come in and request a certain server, their table should be considered a bonus for the server and not be counted toward the number of guests when using the counting method. You would want to check the restaurant's policy on this.

Of course, the guests understand that if they request a certain server and that server is busy, they may have to wait a bit until the server is finished with the other guests.

Seating guests

Seating takes planning. When looking at the seating chart, try to come up with two or more possible places to seat guests depending on which server is up next and the number of people in the party. That way, when guests object to the first table they are taken to, you can lead them to another table. Try to make sure that the other table is in the same section originally assigned to the server, or take them to the next server in line. Then, when the next party needs to be seated, try to seat them with the original server.

If you are seating a large party in a server's section, and another table is still available in the same section, check with the server to see if he or she is ready to take on another party before seating a second party, or if it would be better to wait a little. The server would be in a better position to give good service to both parties. This can also be explained to the waiting guests.

When taking guests to a table, walk slowly and pace your steps to those of the guests. Otherwise, you could leave them behind trying to catch up or lose them completely. It is a good policy to talk to the guests while leading them to their table. Chatting about the weather, giving them compliments on their wardrobe, or asking if they have been to the restaurant before, etc. will make the guests feel welcome and put them at ease when they have to walk some distance to the table.

If you find out that the guests are in the restaurant for the first time, tell the server, so he or she can give them the full introduction routine.

Be careful not to put words into the guest's mouth by asking, "Is this table OK?" They may just say "No" and ask for a table in another section. Then the server who was supposed to attend to them would lose his or her guests. Asking the guests if they want to sit at a table or in a booth while you are still at the host stand is fine as long as they are in the station with the next-in-line server. Most guests will request a booth, and knowing this, the host can try to fill all booths up going from one server section to another. Then seating the tables will be much easier.

Many times people come in and will seat themselves wherever they want to sit. Then you have a problem. You can always try to inform the guests that it may take longer for them to get service because they chose a table in a section that had been just recently sat with guests who had come in before them. If this is the case, this explanation will help give the server some time before having to attend to them without the guests complaining. Servers should still acknowledge them. If the guests don't want to wait, you can suggest another table where you had planned to seat them in the first place. This suggestion is made to make sure the guests get the best possible service, their approval, and their understanding.

If the restaurant is not busy and guests want to sit in a closed section, the host or the manager would have to assign another server to it. If the restaurant is too busy and no other server is available to pick up the table, the host should inform the incoming guests and put them on a short wait-list.

This is not the ideal situation, but it does happen, and the one thing everyone must know is that once a party is seated, they will want to be served promptly no matter if it was stated that it might take time to get served.

On top of the counting system, when you are looking at the floor sections, try to seat people in a server's section that is least busy, or, in other words, has more tables available. This may throw off the counting system a little bit, but the guests will get better service. I have seen many times completely full sections, and at the same time there were one or two empty sections. What happens in that case? When guests come in to be seated, the host has only those one or two empty sections available and then those two servers get "double or triple seated." This is not a good practice.

Once the guests are all seated, present each one with an open menu, starting with the ladies, and mention any specials which are being offered. If you have the time, point out certain areas in the menu — such as where the appetizers are listed — and show them other menus on the table like the dessert menu, kids' menu, or wine list and tell them who their server is going to be.

Also, bring a highchair or sling, if needed, and remove any extra settings that will not be needed. The guests will have more room on the table, and it will save time in polishing and/or rolling silverware.

Before leaving say, "Enjoy your meal!" Don't just walk away.

Once you are done with the seating and the restaurant seems to be getting busier, do an open menu count.

Open menus

Open menus are all of the menus that are on the tables in front of guests who still have to order. You must understand how many open menus the kitchen can handle. In the next three stages, the kitchen can handle up to 40 open menus.

1. If the kitchen has only 10 or so open menus, you can go ahead and seat new people coming in.

2. If the kitchen has 20 to 30 open menus, slow down the pace and try to keep the kitchen from "going under." (Try not to go to the next stage at this point.)

3. If the kitchen is "going under" when there are over 40 open menus, everybody in the kitchen will be moving as fast as they can, which is a sure sign that they have a lot of orders to get ready and cannot handle any more.

Once the range of open menus is known, you need to learn to stick to that range, or, at least, close to it. The number will vary from one situation to another depending on the parties and the number of people they are still waiting to join them. To get a more accurate count, it would be better not to seat people until everyone is there. This will help guide you to slow down with seating people or to pick up seating if necessary.

If more than one host is on duty, the host in charge of seating the guests should relay information to the main host so he or she can decide either to go on a false wait or to stretch out the normal wait time.

If the kitchen is "going under" (Stage 3), you can help them by dragging your feet. While walking back to the host stand, you should look around to see if every guest has been greeted by a server. If not, or you are not sure, go to the table and ask. If the server has not yet been to the table and taken the drink orders, offer to get them something to drink. Otherwise, if they would like bar beverages, locate the server.

The kitchen "going under" means that the kitchen has too many orders to process quickly and effectively. They are overwhelmed.

To further help the kitchen, you could walk slowly to and from tables and follow some steps shown on the checklist in the Appendix, then go back to the host stand. Maybe you would not want to do all the things that are listed on the checklist because, if you do, the main host on duty will not see you for an hour or so!

Wait time

Many hosts want to seat guests the minute they enter the restaurant as long as there is a table available, and some places accept this no matter how busy the restaurant is. That puts a lot of pressure on the kitchen and can lead to guest dissatisfaction. It would be more beneficial to go on a wait, if needed.

Here are a few reasons why:

- Once guests park their cars and walk in, they most likely will not leave and go anywhere else when you tell them that it will take just five or ten minutes before they can be seated. It also gives them the impression that this establishment must be a really good place to eat.

- Going on a short wait will help the servers and the kitchen staff catch up if they fall behind. A few extra minutes can make a world of difference for service and guest satisfaction.

Here are a few guidelines for estimating the wait times more accurately.

1. You first have to look at how many tables are available and the size of the tables. Most parties will be ready to leave after about an hour or an hour and a half from the time they were seated. Large parties tend to stay much longer and talk. A big part to figure into the equation is also to observe at what stage of service every table is in. For example, find out which guests were just recently seated and are still on their drinks, which party is currently eating, or which tables have guests eating their desserts with already packed to-go boxes.

Example of a wait sheet:

Time arrived	Name	Number in party	Quote Time	Possible Table*

* "Possible table" means that you see a table which may be available either for a large or a small party. This can be any table shown in the floor plan you would consider to seat with a new party but have not yet done so.

2. There are computer programs available which can be used to help. It will show on the computer how long guests are at a table. For example, if a party has been there for 50 minutes, the wait time can probably be quoted as 10 to 15 minutes based on the above information.

3. Give the guests a small timespan, like 10 to 15 minutes, and don't just say that it will take 10 minutes. Giving a time span allows more "wiggle room." If you give them 10 minutes, the guest surely will be back asking for the table and stating that they were told 10 minutes. Yes, this happens, unfortunately.

4. When trying to estimate the wait time, you should also look at the number of tickets the kitchen has to see if they are backed up or can get the food out in a timely fashion, do an open menu check, and check on the servers to see when they are ready to take on another table or if they are still too busy.

5. Another way to quote a wait time is to add three to five extra minutes to the estimated wait time for tables with parties that are less than four people. For example, if you need a four-top, you add three to five minutes to the wait time; if you need two four-tops, you add six to 10 minutes to the wait time; etc. Try not to quote over an hour unless you know that tables are not flipping, or unless you have a very long line. Wouldn't that be wonderful to see?

Outside seating

When the establishment uses an outdoor patio, make sure that, before opening it to guests, the tables are ready, aligned, clean, and dry (if it has rained recently); that they are set up with all the items the inside tables may have (for instance, check often-overlooked items such as salt and pepper); and that servers are assigned to them.

Once everything is ready, ask every party coming in if they prefer inside or outside seating, if tables outside are still available. If not, and the guests still want to sit outside, they will need to be put on an outside wait-list.

There are three problems with outside seating for the guests:

1. Too much sun. If it happens that there are some tables without an umbrella, it may be too hot to sit outside and eat.

2. It's too cold outside, and some tables don't have heating units. Then, of course, not only are people getting cold but so is the food.

3. If it looks like it may rain and the guests want to come inside later, tables may not be available for them, unless a section is set aside for this reason.

Knowing which tables have umbrellas and/or heaters and warning the guests of all those possibilities might change their minds and will be beneficial for the hosts when they are seating people.

Phone seating

There are different types of phone seating: "Heads' Up," "Call Ahead," and "Reservations."

1. **Heads' Up:**

   Guests will call the restaurant to let them know that they will be coming in with a large group. This is giving the restaurant a heads' up and is not a reservation or a call ahead.

   A heads' up call does not guarantee that the group will be seated right away. It merely helps you and the servers to plan their best to accommodate them without taking too much time away from the servers already taking care of the other tables. Knowing that a large group will be coming, you can determine where to seat them without holding tables for an extended amount of time, or waiting for other guests to leave and decide if and what tables you have to put together.

   If guests do not give the restaurant a heads' up call before they are coming in with a large group, the hosts will not be ready to accommodate them by having an idea where to put them. You may have to stop seating guests in a server's section in order to put tables together. This would leave the server with nothing to do until the party can be seated. Many times the people at a table needed for the party will talk and talk and not leave for a long time after they are done eating. When this happens, the party is usually seated in another section. In one of the places I worked, they actually stopped seating in two different areas, resulting in two or more servers being idle for more than an hour.

2. Call Ahead (CA):

If the restaurant practices call ahead seating, make sure that the guests understand how it works, and tell the guests that it is not a reservation. When the guests call, you enter their name and the number of people in the party into a computer or on a CA sheet. When the restaurant goes on a wait, you transfer their names to the wait-list marked with a symbol "CA" to show that they had called ahead. When the guests arrive, you can either seat them at the next available table, or you can give them a pager and information on how long it may take for them to get seated. You must make sure that the time they called is written down to be able to place their name in order on a wait-list.

3. Reservations:

When taking a reservation, you have to guarantee that a table is available to the guest for a certain time and for the number of people given. Do not take a reservation for a large party without talking to the manager first unless the manager says that it is OK. All reservations should be immediately put into the reservation book.

A few things to keep in mind when taking the reservation:

- Check the date and time the guest wants to make the reservation for and the number of people in the party to make sure that they can be accommodated. If it is for a holiday, a manager may have to approve it. Always take down a phone number! This number can come in handy when the guests are running late. You can call them to find out if they still intend to come, or it allows you to notify them when something happens in the restaurant. I worked at a place that had a power outage. The manager called all the guests who had made a reservation and told them not to come in because the restaurant could not serve any food. They also offered them a discount on their next reservation.

- If a reservation was made and the party does not show up, or does not call within 15 minutes of the appointed time, and you tried and could not reach them, use the table for other guests, if needed. If they do show up later, the manager can explain and handle the situation.

- On the day of the reservation, you must make sure that the table is set up and that the server is aware of the people coming in. This will help the server to make any needed preparations.

- The establishment should have reservation guidelines to go by. An example is: For every two people allow one hour eating time, for every four people allow one and a half hours, and if there are more than four people in the party allow two to two and a half hours eating time depending on the number of people. Hopefully, the next guests coming in will understand if they have to wait a bit when the party does not leave within that time frame. The hours in your estimate may differ.

High-tops

When you must go on a normal wait because there are no more seats available, always recommend tables that are not in the rotation of seating. For example, many restaurants have high-tops. Those tables are in the bar area and can seat two to four people comfortably. Most restaurants do not use those tables in any kind of rotation. They are available on a first come, first serve basis. Many people don't know about those tables and mentioning them can help you to get off the wait-list.

False wait

A "false wait" is when the restaurant has tables available for seating and puts people on a wait because the kitchen cannot handle any more orders and needs some time to catch up.

In this case, it also is important for you to let the bartender know that they are on a wait so they do not take any meal orders. I have seen people go to the bar and place their order with the bartender; this does not help the kitchen.

This situation also applies to any guests seated at high-tops. The servers for those tables should be aware of this and also not take the orders right away.

Conclusion

In this position you learn about table numbers, the importance of communication with co-workers, the location of everything in the restaurant, and problems associated with the position. This gives you a good foundation to proceed to the 'take-out' position.

Part Three

Take-Out Service, Servers, and Bartenders

Chapter 5

Take-Out Service

he most important part in handling take-out orders is accuracy. To be accurate, you need to have menu knowledge, computer knowledge, know a bit about guest relations, and have organizational skills.

Make sure that all of the items that were ordered, for example: steak, mashed potatoes, broccoli, etc. are cooked as the guest had specified (that the steak is medium, the broccoli is soft, etc.) and are in the bag. You also have to be sure that all the extras like bread, if the restaurant includes it without charge; ketchup; silverware; salt; pepper; napkins; etc. have been added. Proper stocking of all the accompanying items will expedite these tasks. It would be a good idea if the person taking the order would ask the guest if they want or need the accompanying items. Many times guests don't want or need certain items that usually come with the orders and just toss them out. I have talked to guests who specifically state each time they order that they do not want certain accompaniments, but get them anyhow. What a waste!

Knowledge of the menu is a must to be able to answer the guests' questions when they are placing their orders. Keeping a menu in front of you when taking the order, especially if you are new to the job, will help. If you are not sure, do *not* make up an answer. A better way is to ask the guest to please wait a moment so you can find out. In this position, you will learn, for instance, what is in a sauce and what it would go with, how things taste so you can describe it to the guests, and what items can be substituted to suit the guests' taste.

Computer knowledge is important when it comes to speed and understanding, as well as in taking orders. It is good to know where all the buttons are located (speed) and in what order the buttons have to be pressed (understanding). For example, the temperature button for a steak might be before the button for a potato. (See later sections in this part and Part Four: Managers.)

When the guests pick up their order, make sure they check the items in the bag before they leave to confirm that it contains everything they ordered. This allows them to point out if something is missing, or to have something added they might have overlooked. This also prevents people from calling later on saying that they did not receive an item they ordered.

The take-out service represents the restaurant to the outside world, and it is very important for you to understand this. If something goes wrong with the order — for instance, the utensils were not included, or any other items are missing, things cannot be corrected as they can be when it happens in the restaurant. The better the take-out service is, the more sales can be made. To become good in this job, you can always ask co-workers for advice and learn from them.

Conclusion

In this position a to-go person can increase their knowledge about the menu, the computer system, and gain come insight to guest service. You will now be ready to proceed to serving where you will learn more about how to read a guest, steps of service, and much more.

Chapter 6

Servers

Introduction

Being a server is one of the most difficult positions in the front of the house (FOH) — i.e., not back in the kitchen. Not only does a server have to perform the required tasks, but also has to deal with various personalities of the public from gracious people to downright rude people; and to top it all off, a server may also have to deal with all kinds of problems and complaints. A term used in this profession is "Work smarter, not harder!" A server has to communicate, work together with others, and always has to think of how to solve a problem or make a task easier, such as keeping the folded side of beverage napkins facing either up or forward, so they are easier to grab.

No matter where you work, you alone, based on the service you give, have an impact on how much money you can earn. The exception, of course, is when business is slow and when the restaurant does not have enough guests.

To become a professional server requires a lot of work, concentration, and knowledge. It is a profession. No matter what the circumstances are, the job should be treated as a profession, not just as a job to make a quick buck.

The topics in this chapter are shown in alphabetical order. They will give general information and suggestions that can be used throughout a working shift.

86 board

The term "86" is used most frequently in restaurants. It means that the establishment is out of a certain item. The restaurant may have an "86 board," or it may be part of their computer system. Some places just use the term verbally. The "86" term is one of the more important terms listed under "terminology" in the back of this book.

The term "86" is mentioned in many places. Nobody really knows where it originated. The one guess I like is that it came from the movie industry. When shooting a film in color, a camera needs an "85 filter" (amber) to balance the daylight. When shooting indoors under tungsten light, the filter is either removed or replaced with a clear filter. The clear filter, or no filter at all, was referred to as the "86" filter meaning "nothing" or "get rid of."

Arriving at work

Upon arrival, let the manager know that you are in and ready to work. This may sound trivial, but because some people do not take their jobs seriously and think that they can come and go as they please, it would give the manager piece of mind to know that everyone scheduled to work showed up. It also lets the manager know how responsible a person is and gives him or her a good idea of who to keep on staff and who to let go.

Come fully dressed in your appropriate uniform, check your attire for any accidental dirt spots or stains, spit out any gum, listen to any pre-shift staff meetings, and then proceed to the section assigned to you. You want to check the tables, chairs, and the floors around your section to see that they are clean; check the salt and pepper shakers to make sure that they are clean and filled; see that the tables are set with silverware and napkins or any other appropriate items; and check the knives and forks for spots or any food particles still stuck to them. This is hard to do if the establishment rolls silverware. Then the items should be checked before rolling them. These simple things help to avoid guest dissatisfaction and to keep tips up.

Buddy system

This system is most helpful to all servers. When you are assigned to a section, find out who is serving next to you. It could be either one or two people. Knowing who your "buddies" are can help in multiple ways: you can watch their tables when they have to go to the bathroom or on a break; you can lend an extra eye and can help refill drinks and take dirty plates; and serve desserts or other food items when they are occupied elsewhere — and vice versa. You also can answer guests' questions and fetch items even when those guests are not assigned to you. Being able to ask a buddy to help out when you are in the weeds gives you that extra hand or two. This is called teamwork and creates unity.

Checkbooks

When you are finished with a checkbook, make sure to remove any slips, and check that it is clean and ready to be used again.

Try not to use the guest checkbooks as your writing book to enter orders, but if you do, please do not take them home. If this ever happens, make sure that you bring them back. One of the restaurants I worked for showed the restaurant logo on the checkbooks. I guess they became a collector's item, because after about a week we had a hard time finding one to use for the guests, which made our job harder to do.

Condiments

Never marry condiments! It is disgusting to keep putting new stuff on top of older stuff and usage never gets to the bottom. Not only is marrying condiments a big health risk, but it is also against the health codes, and the restaurant can be fined when caught by one of OSHA's agents upon inspection. Now I understand why guests always ask for a new bottle every time they go out to eat! Such things as A1, ketchup, mustard, or any other liquid items should be used down to the bottom of the bottle. When a bottle is almost empty, you could either bring a new one with the old one and ask the guest to please finish off the old one before opening the new bottle, or take the nearly empty bottle to the back for servers or cooks to use, either for cooking or on their own food. Some restaurants use "bullets" to put these condiments in, thereby eliminating the issue.

Any condiment containers that need to be filled on a daily basis such as salt, pepper, and sugar caddies, should be emptied at least once a week, or more, and the containers should be cleaned before they are refilled. Those containers should also be wiped down after every guest leaves and before new guests are seated to prevent a bad experience. Let's face it — would anyone want to grab a salt and pepper shaker that may have dried barbeque or buffalo sauce on it? Yuck!

Customer needs

If a guest in the restaurant, other than a guest you are presently serving, asks for something, just get it. Trying to go and look for the other server is just a waste of time, not only for you, but also for the guest. If the guest asks for an alcoholic drink and you cannot order it, tell the guest that you will let their server know right away, or, if possible, ask the bartender to make the drink and have the server ring it in as a "don't make."

Always watch guests to see if they are looking around. Usually, this means they need something, or they are looking for the server. Then you can offer your assistance. Every once in a while you will have a guest who says that he or she is just looking around. This is a great opportunity for you to strike up a conversation, making him or her feel welcome and more at home, especially if the guest is not at one of your tables. You do understand the reason for this, right? Next time, this guest might just ask for you.

Dishland

If the establishment has you bring the dirty dishes back to the dish area to be washed, make sure that all food items are scraped off or dumped and plates of the same size are placed on top of each other. This helps with the stacking and makes the area less congested. It also helps the dishwashers and kitchen staff to clean and retrieve plates more quickly.

If dishes are put into a bus bin, which I do not recommend, you have to make sure that all food items are scraped off or dumped for the same reason as above. If there are three bins in a cart, putting all glasses, small items like "monkey dishes," and silverware in the top bin followed by plates in the bottom two bins will help the dishwasher to work faster.

A monkey dish is a small dish used for sauces, butter, or other small items.

Emptying something

The worst thing — OK, maybe not the worst thing, but it is right up there — is emptying something and not refilling it or at least telling somebody to help refill it.

This only seems to happen when people are too busy and the contents are needed; it could be coffee, bread, ice, kids' cups, butter, etc. Everybody on the floor needs to work together and make sure that these popular items are always available. Some places assign people to refill these items as part of their side work, but it does not matter; everyone who finds the time should do it.

Also, when a last item is taken from storage like ketchup, straws, cups, etc., the manager should be notified. Management may not have been aware that the last item was used, and these are things the restaurant would not want to run out of. OK, in an ideal work environment managers would be right on top of this, but if not, try to help them out. They have a lot to do.

Expo

Most restaurants have some sort of "Expedite" or "Expo," a person who helps to get food ready when it comes from the kitchen. They are located by the kitchen windows opposite the cooks, and as the kitchen finishes food items, the expo gets items such as sauces that go with the dishes; adds condiments, such as butter and sour cream to baked potatoes; get sthe au jus for a prime rib roast; adds extra plates if needed; and places everything on service trays, when trays are being used. Once everything in an order is ready, the expo has the food runners or the servers bring it out to the tables.

The job the "expos" are doing prevents a lot of chaos in the kitchen because all servers must go to the expo if they need anything from the kitchen. Can you imagine what it would be like if eight servers would call for different items at the same time? It is much easier if only one person can say: "Hey Joe, I need three of this (or four of that)!" instead of the servers calling for each item they needed. In some restaurants, the expos also pack up take-out orders and have them ready to go. This person makes sure that servers get what they need, but also makes sure that extra food is not being served.

"On the fly" is a term used when mistakes happen and the item is needed like "yesterday," such as: a server submitting a wrong food item or dropping the item, or by the cooks not preparing it properly and having to re-make the dish. The request to the kitchen would be "I need this on the fly." On the computer, the server types in "fly," and the manager or expo should be able to "bump that ticket" to the front and take care of it personally. This will help prevent more dissatisfaction by the guest and allow the manager or expo to fix the problem at the table.

In one place I worked, neither the expo, the manager, or the server could get these "fly" kitchen items out any faster because the ticket was never placed in the front. The items came out just like placing the order the first time. The cooks simply prepare the food in line with all the other entrees. This, of course, should never be acceptable.

Famous or well-known people

In some cases, you may have the opportunity to serve a well-known or important person. But no matter who it is, the attention to detail and level of service should not change. Every guest should be treated in the same exceptional manner.

When Mrs. Hillary Clinton was campaigning with her husband, the entire family stayed at the hotel where I was working. I served lunch to Mr. Clinton and a group of seven people. Everyone asked me how I was doing and if I was nervous. I told them, "No." I treated Mr. Clinton just like any other guest, and he appreciated it.

The one philosophy I use is that, just because someone has a well-known face and name, he or she is not any different than the rest of us humans. He or she still puts his or her pants on one leg at a time, becomes sick occasionally, and goes to the bathroom (to put it politely). We all deserve to be treated like stars!

This philosophy could also apply when serving a general manager, regional manager, or corporate manager in your establishment. As long as you are doing your job to the best of your ability, you should not have to worry or become nervous.

First In, First Out (FIFO)

FIFO applies to everything in the restaurant, but some things are sometimes overlooked such as to-go boxes. Many servers, when they are doing their side work, will stack new to-go boxes on top of old ones. What will happen is that the staff never gets to use the boxes on the bottom of the stack, kind of like the salt and pepper shakers, which always have to be full and are never emptied. Boxes can collect dust or become extremely dirty from being moved around the counter so much where food or drinks get spilled. Rotating these items will help you when someone forgets to order more and you have to use the last one.

Foreigners

Not everyone we serve is from the U.S. and is familiar with the standard tipping procedures. Most of the time foreigners do not leave a tip. Heck! Even people who live in this country don't always tip properly, if at all. What some servers do not always realize is that other countries have different customs, and the people from those countries are not familiar with our ways. In Europe, for instance, the tip is built into the total food or drink costs and paid out later with the wages. Those guests usually round up the amount of their total bill and give the server "a little extra" on the side to show their appreciation for any good service. They just don't know any better, unless they read their travel guides. For our servers, it just is not right. Everyone should study his or her travel documents before traveling to different regions in the world to learn about customs in their destination country. That includes us when we travel! But the servers cannot tell them that. (See "Teaching the public" in Chapter 6.)

Full hands in, and full hands out

It means just what it states, always having something in your hands. The concept should become second nature to you. When leaving the kitchen, you bring out such things as food, glasses, drinks, restock items (which are many), etc. When entering the kitchen, you carry dirty dishes, glasses, trays and stands either from the tables you are serving or from someone else's table. Always look around to see what needs to be done.

Nobody at the host stand

When guests walk into the restaurant and there is no one in sight to greet them, you would want to do it. If you do not have the time, tell the guests that the host will be right back to assist them. Acknowledging a guest is the key to good customer service.

Also, when the phone is unattended, you would want to answer it. Know what to say when picking up the phone and listen carefully. If you can assist the caller, then do so, but if you cannot assist the caller, then put the caller on hold so you can find someone who can. Try not to let the phone ring more than twice.

Odd things

You need to keep in mind that there are things you may see which don't make sense to you. For instance: the hosts may be putting small tables together for a large party while a big table is already set up and available. It could be that the large table is being held for another party, or they simply requested to sit there. We don't always know what's going on at the host station —same goes when the hosts double seat or skip a server. Sometimes guests tell the host where they want to sit when they come in.

Once, as a manager, I had to put a large round table together with a small two-top square table. A server came in and proceeded to take it apart. When I pulled her aside and asked why she was doing it, she said "Because it looks stupid." I agreed, but that was something the guests had requested, and sometimes we have to do things to make the guests happy, no matter what.

Problem-solving

Servers, who have worked in this profession for a long time know that problems with guests always come up, but how they handle those problems and in what way they talk to the guests will have the guests come back or not. The guests do not care who or what caused the problem. They are only interested in how it is being resolved. One thing is to never try and push it away or blame others for it. Accept the problem, if allowed — and resolve it yourself or ask for help from the manager.

A former boss once told me that "In most cases you start out with a 25 percent tip, and it goes down from there unless you know what to do, **how to prevent the problem from happening in the first place**, and how to react when a problem does come up." The problem can be as simple as a dirty knife or as complex as a meal that was not cooked properly. How to react will depend on the nature of the problem and the reaction of the guest. For instance: If the meat was overcooked, offering to cook a new piece may be acceptable to one guest but not to another. They may not want to wait. If that is the case, offering something else, which does not take that long to prepare, would be the option.

Here are some suggestions, listed in order:

1. Offer to replace the original item
2. Offer something equivalent to the original item or ask if they would like to look at the menu again
3. Try to offer a dessert if you are allowed to do so
4. Offer to take the meal off the bill
5. If all fails, get a manager. If you solved the problem, tell the manager.

Overall, be sincere that you are willing to fix the problem. If you tried to fix the problem twice and the guest is still not happy, get a manager to help. **Always** let the manager know about every step you took, so that they will be prepared to help.

Running food

Everyone knows what this means; but if or when you have to do it, you have to be 100 percent positive that you are "running" the right dishes. The most important thing you must do when you are not 100 percent sure is to **ASK**. To run the correct item is important because, if the wrong item is run, not only does the guest receive something he or she did not order, but also another guest, for whom the item was intended, will have to wait for the kitchen to make a new one. That results in two unhappy guests, the kitchen staff getting angry because they have more work to do, and an increase in food costs because of the waste. Remember: avoid problems in the first place.

A "food runner" is a member of the
restaurant staff that delivers food
to the tables.

Saving steps

Saving steps is an organized discipline. You do a lot of running back and forth. In order to save steps, you need to be able to either look at the tables assigned to you or at your book to determine what (if anything) each table needs. Once you know what every table needs, you can collect all the items and distribute them at the different tables. If you cannot do this in one trip, you should organize it so you can do it in two trips. For instance: if you are able to get all the alcoholic drinks in one trip, you would only have to go to the bar once, then you can get the bread and butter and all nonalcoholic drinks in the second trip.

Many times guests will ask for an item, and when you bring it they ask for additional items. To eliminate this back and forth try to take a moment, look around the table, and ask them if they may need other specific items. For instance, someone asks for more ketchup. You look around the table and spot the hot tea kettle. You would want to ask if they may need more hot water. That will prevent you from having to make multiple runs. Saving steps can come in handy when you are really busy.

Sayings/terms

Behind — It is very important to remember to say "Behind" whenever you go behind another person. Letting people know where you are when moving around in the restaurant is a courtesy to everyone when heavy trays and glassware are being lifted and tossed about. Calling "Behind" can save food, drinks, and avoid unnecessary accidents.

Heard — If the kitchen needs something like certain kinds of plates, etc., and the cooks call for them, the term "Heard" is used to confirm that someone not only heard, but also will get the items needed.

Corner — Another term servers sometimes use when going in or out of the kitchen is "Corner" to avoid crashing into each other when they cannot see the other person, especially when carrying loaded trays.

No Problem — This saying is used way too often. So, try not to use it. It can indicate that there was a problem to begin with, which may not have been the case. Saying instead "That will be fine, sure" or "I can do that" is better.

Shift leaders

A shift leader is a person who has been with the establishment for a certain length of time and knows how everything should be done.

Every server will have some sort of side work to do during and after their shift. The tasks, which need to be done, are put on a list so the shift leader can check out every server's side work at the end of the shift. (There is a sample list in Part Five) This is important for the smooth running of a restaurant. If someone did not do his or her side work, the people working the next shift would have to make up for it. It will be hard on everybody, makes everyone angry, and cuts down efficiency.

When it is time to get checked out, some places have the shift leader sign a slip, or just have him or her sign a report. At the end, the manager should be checking out the shift leader to ensure that all of the work was completed.

Shift-leading is not as hard as it sounds. If the staff works well together, they will all do what is expected.

I would tell a new person that I would trust him or her to do the assigned side work and sign the report without actually checking if he or she did it. But if the person failed to do it, and I had to do it instead, I would not trust him or her anymore. It happened only once. This person had to wait until I had a chance to check his or her work, meanwhile, I was signing others off right away and they were able to go home. After approximately two months the person came to me, apologized, and asked for another chance, which I granted. The person had learned the hard way and never failed to complete the work again.

Sneezing and coughing

Every now and then you cannot prevent this from happening. You just have to remember never to use your hands to stop a sneeze or a cough. You can use the corner of an elbow instead. That way the germs do not get on your hands and guests will feel more comfortable when you resume your work.

Soda machine

When the machine runs out of a certain type of soda, push up the front panel. This will let others know that the item is out of stock or needs to be replaced. It saves time and prevents dumping out good ice.

Talking among staff members

When they are talking together in stations, many servers do not think that the guests in the restaurant can overhear them. They are wrong, even though they would not want their guests to listen to them — especially if the conversations are inappropriate, for example, they are complaining about other guests not leaving enough tips, problems at work or at home, or blame others for things that went wrong with another server, host, or the kitchen. Guests do not need to hear this.

And we should not forget about talking in the bathrooms. Anyone can overhear there, too.

Here is a funny story. One day, when I was cleaning the high chairs and booster chairs that were next to the bathroom, I overheard two ladies in the bathroom talking about their husbands and things they could not perform anymore. When they came out of the restroom and saw me laughing, they turned red and asked if I overheard them. I said, "Yes, I am sorry, I did not mean to." They laughed and said: "That's OK, you don't know our husbands, so this will stay between us girls."

And this is a sad story. A server was complaining about his or her guests, and these same guests overheard the conversation. The guest in turn complained to the manager, and the server was fired.

Many guests also do not like to be seated close to the kitchen because of the traffic in and out, and the loud noise. They don't want to hear a server yell, "I need another steak because this one is overcooked," or any other shouts. So, for these tables try to keep the noise level down. You may end up serving that table one day.

I was working one day, standing in the middle of the restaurant talking to my guests, when everybody in the dining room heard the manager yell from the kitchen for the staff to stop talking and to run food instead. Of course, talking among staff members is cause for frustration and anger for the manager, but yelling at them that loudly is not acceptable. Even the guests were stunned by what they heard.

Be careful when talking to each other because voices can carry farther than you realize.

Talking with guests

When you are chatting with your guests try to avoid discussing politics, religion, and especially not problems the restaurant may have. Keep personal opinions to yourself as much as possible. Safer topics to talk about are, for instance, where they are from, whether they grew up there, places they have been, and things they have seen. If the guests talk about other things, just listen and agree, even you don't. If they ask for your opinion, you could just say something like "I'm not sure" or "Maybe." If you get the chance, you could try to bring up the talk about wages as mentioned below in the paragraph "Teaching the public."

Never lie to guests or say something that is (for lack of a better word) stupid. For instance, if they ask, "Can I have avocado, please?" you should not say, "Sorry, we have it, but it's not prepared." Check with a manager, and if the item is available, just get it. Let the guests know, however, that there might be an up-charge before ordering the item.

People can see right through a lie, and, sometimes, even if it is not a lie, they do not believe it, or they don't care. Try to get whatever the guests requested, in all ways possible, and be honest about something you may have done wrong. For instance, that you forgot to put in their order and that is the reason why it is taking so long.

Teaching the public

There is a sneaky way to teach your guests to become better tippers. Whenever the conversation with guests comes up about buying this or that, you can simply state, "Yeah, like I can afford something like that on $____ an hour."

Many people, even businessmen, may not know that in most places, servers receive less than minimum wage and have to make up the rest of their income with tips. Their response is usually: "Really? That is all you make?" When you give guests this information, you are helping all other servers in the industry.

I once talked to a businessman about a Ferrari and jokingly said, "Yeah, like I can afford to buy one making $3.21 per hour." He nearly choked. He was so taken aback, realizing that, all the times that he ate at restaurants he was leaving only a token tip. He vowed that from that day on he would always leave a 20 percent tip or more. I thanked him and received a 50 percent tip from him that day.

I have also been able to tell guests how some restaurants handle tips. Some take a deduction from a server's paycheck as a tip-out amount, and others encourage a server to tip out a certain percentage to the hosts, bartenders, food runners, bussers, or a combination of all. So, a server never receives the entire 15-25 percent tip the guests may leave. We all know that if we don't tip out, we don't receive any help from those quarters. They are giving you a service, just like you are giving service to your guests. Letting the guest know if you have to tip out gives them a better understanding about how things work in the industry.

Teamwork

When people think of teamwork, they think teamwork is only a way of accomplishing things. It's a helping hand when needed, a way to make things easier, a feeling of being a big part in something, and belonging to a group of people who have the same ideas, beliefs, and values. But it's more than that. It's a state of mind. Think of everything you do. Do you do it for yourself? For your co-workers? The answer is no. You do it not just to help each other but also for the guests and the successful operation of the restaurant. Teamwork is everything that is important in the field of hospitality!

Teamwork should not just be done in the front of the house (FOH) or just in the back of the house (BOH), but it should be done in both places together. Without everyone working together, things can easily fall apart. The little things people do for each other add up to great accomplishments in the end.

I once opened a restaurant where, of course, everyone was in the same boat. We all relied on each other to get things done. The unique thing about this place was that all the workers went above basics. We worked so well together as a team that our guests would come back just to watch us. They even told us that it was like we were putting on a show. As one person was clearing a table and then began chatting with the guests, another would come by to take the dirty plates right out of his or her hands, so the server could keep talking in comfort — and the server never reacted. It was almost like it was expected. If we could not refill glasses ourselves, we would mention it. Someone, who happened to have the time, would do it. This practice in teamwork was the norm for us. Some things were not expected of us, but it was something we all understood and did for each other. (See the appendix.) Just by observing, servers can come up with their own ideas and jump into action whenever the need arises.

Just for your information: if teamwork does not work and staff members have a hard time keeping up with side work, management may hire and schedule more people on the floor and assign fewer tables to each server to make sure these things get done; so, servers want to be careful if they don't want management to do that.

Teamwork cannot work if only one or two people do it. Everybody around has to participate. If there is not enough teamwork practiced in the establishment, you can try to follow the list in the appendix on your own and hope that others will catch on and start doing the same. As the saying goes, "Lead by example." If others see it done, they may follow. Always doing something for others tends to get reciprocated. It's human nature!

It will also be helpful and create a friendlier atmosphere if you learn the names of the kitchen employees. It is so much more personal when you say, "Hey Mitch, can I get a side of mayo, please," instead of yelling, "I need a side of mayo." Even "Please" does not soften it enough. Also, remember that they may be so focused on what they are doing that they may not even hear you. So, calling their name will get their attention. (See "Expo" earlier on in this chapter.)

Tips

Tips are a private thing and should not be broadcasted — neither should anyone ask. You can receive outstanding tips from some guests when you do your job well, but at the same time you may not receive much from others. But at the end it all seems to average out.

Don't ever swear over a bad tip, especially in the dining room when closing out your check. That can get you fired, especially if a guest overhears you. (Like in "Talking among staff members.") Receiving a bad tip and telling others about it can give others the impression that you are a bad server and will not get any sympathy.

Tools that servers need

An apron should be given to servers upon hiring. Additional ones may have to be purchased.

A) At least five pens, one you use to write the orders with and the rest to leave at the tables for the guests to use to sign their credit card slips, based on a four-table section. Do not carry any of the pens in the hair or behind the ear. That is just tacky and used on TV only with no concept of sanitation. Carry more pens, if needed, since these get misplaced or taken by guests occasionally.

B) A "bank" of about $30.00, which should include coins and small bills, to use when change is needed, so you do not have to rely on another server or cashier. This also helps save time and extra steps. The "bank" should be put into a pocket, zipper bag, coin bag, or a small makeup bag.

C) A book or notepad for writing down orders should not be stuck in the back of the pants (believe me, I have seen this done) — only in aprons. Never put bills into a book or pad where they can easily fall out.

A server was pulling out a piece of paper from his book while walking back to the kitchen, and with it came a $100 bill that fell on the floor. Luckily, being a trainer at the time, I happened to be following him. I picked it up and held onto it until the end of our shift. That's when he realized he was short on money. I gave him back the money and, yes, he learned his lesson.

D) A lighter to light candles in case the guests celebrate a birthday, an anniversary, or another special event.

E) Not required, but handy: mini flashlights can be used in darkly lit restaurants, especially for elderly patrons who may have eye problems. They also come in handy for the preparation of a steak and its viability. When using a flashlight, you can show the guests (and yourself) the true temperature of the meat. In one of the steak houses I worked at, we did this often. You would be surprised how many times a steak looked like it was well done, when it actually was medium rare!

F) In fancier establishments, servers also should carry a wine opener and a crumber — and know how to use them.

G) Butt rags. These are linen napkins that servers use to handle hot plates, for wiping tables, or for cleaning their fingers. Originally these were kitchen rags, and eventually they were replaced by napkins, but keeping the same name. If the establishment allows the use of them, they should always be replaced whenever they are dirty. Having guests see a napkin hanging from the server with butter stains or sauces like marinara all over it is a sure turn-off for them. Always having a clean napkin is essential to show guests that the restaurant is a clean place to eat. It presents professionalism and pride. Many places even have servers put them in their pockets now instead of hanging on the apron, sometimes you don't know that they are dirty. In this case, another server could be of assistance. No extra eye-lingering, please!

A crumber is a tool you slide across the table to remove crumbs.

Training others

This is one of the most important tasks you may have to perform once you are with the establishment long enough, know all the ins and outs, and, of course, are willing to. You have to understand the training material and practice every step, not just say: "This is what it says, but I don't do it," or "Do as I say, not as I do." That would call for disaster.

Everyone should be trained in the same manner, with the same rules, and with the same guidelines. If one or more rules or guidelines do not work anymore, are obsolete, or needs changing to keep up with changes in the restaurant, then management should review it with the training servers.

The main focus when training someone is to *go slowly*, especially on the computer. As a trainer, you tend to work at a fast pace because it has become second nature to you. You do not realize that a new person does not know everything yet, or simply cannot keep up.

People who worked many years in the industry do not need to concentrate on how to greet a guest, approach a table, or holding a tray. They only need to concentrate on the computer and menu items. People new to the industry have to learn from scratch.

As a trainer, you must allow a new person to do as much as he or she is comfortable with. The more hands-on the person is, the faster he or she will learn and be ready to be on the floor by himself or herself. Make sure that, at the end of each shift, you go through all of the paperwork and show the trainees what needs to be done.

Even while writing this book I realized many times, that in certain places, I forgot to tell you about things most people in the industry know because I took things for granted. I had to re-write some chapters about eight times. I would write at work during my breaks or between shifts, and my mom would later type everything I wrote into the computer. Even so she learned a lot about our industry, she kept asking me questions because she often did not understand what I was talking about. So, my advice is to take it slow, explain everything thoroughly, and always have the trainees ask questions. It's how one learns more. (An example of a Training Program for Servers is in the appendix).

Being able to train other servers should be a goal for every server.

Trays

Trays or tray stands should never be left in the dining room, and if you ever make a mess of a tray, on the top or the bottom, always clean it before putting it back for others to use. Nobody wants to grab a dirty tray and put drinks or food on it, or worse, get sauces all over his or her hands. A used tray should never be put on another clean table either. You can affect three different areas. One, the trays may be wet or have food stuck on the bottom, and now the clean table will be dirty. Two, the host will pass up the table because he or she would not want to seat any new guests at a table with a tray on it. Three, if that table is in another servers' section you have either caused a mess for the other server to clean up or caused him or her to be passed up for a table.

Chapter 7

Steps of Service

I t is a fact that the busier you are, the fewer mistakes you will make. This is because you are more focused on what needs to be done, tend to multitask more, and are more organized. The steps of service is a basic outline of all the things you need to do. Understanding the basic steps will help ensure that your guests have the best service and a wonderful experience.

Step 1: Arrival of Guests

Arrival of Guests:

To make a good first impression, acknowledge incoming guests with eye contact, a smile, or greeting — and be genuine in all aspects during their stay. If you cannot get to them right away say, "I will be right with you."

Greeting the Guests:

If you are not sure what to say when first approaching a table, you could try something like this: "Hi, my name is____, and I will be taking care of you."

Do not call yourself a server, as in, "I will be your server today." In the eyes of the guest this term may put you at a lower status, which of, course, you are not. You are a professional and should be treated as an equal. We say in our industry: "We are ladies and gentlemen serving ladies and gentlemen."

Never call guests terms like "buddies," "fellows," "friends," and especially not "guys," "boys," or "girls" as these terms can be offensive or inappropriate. People may feel insulted by these terms and leave a lower tip. Better terms to use would be "Ma'am," "Sir," "Ladies," or "Gentlemen." You could skip these terms altogether and say just "Good Evening, Afternoon, or Morning" or "Good Evening, everyone."

Once you introduce yourself, you could ask the guests if they have been in before. When the answer is "Yes," you can give them a quick "Welcome Back," and if the answer is "No," you can give them a hearty welcome, proceed to tell them a little about the restaurant and the menu, and suggest popular items. I once said "Welcome Home" instead of "Welcome Back." The guests laughed and said: "Yeah, this really feels like a second home."

Whatever lines you choose to use, never become a "robot" and repeat the same lines in the same way at every table you serve, where every guest can overhear you. Always state your name, though, somewhere during your greeting. You need to read your guests and express your own personality when responding to them and their interests. Acquiring this skill will take time and experience.

If there are any children in the party, make sure that you pay special attention to them. If you can win the kids over, you can win the parents over, and, believe it or not, the parents will go to a restaurant where the children like it the next time they go out to eat. If the kids like you, they will be better behaved, which, in turn, will make the meal more enjoyable for everyone. I know kids can make a mess, but in the long run, taking good care of them will reward you with more money in the pocket and tend to pull in more guests for the restaurant.

Interests:

One way for you to make a connection with your guests is to subtly let them know what your own interests are, which may or may not be the same as your guests. A guest comments on a ring, a necklace, earrings (such as ones with a sport logo), or even a tie, which, for instance, has a keyboard on it (see picture below).

Their words can lead into a mutual, friendly conversation, and at the end they may leave a good tip or an opportunity for you to suggest that they ask for you the next time they come in, helping you build a nice clientele. This might increase your income and bring attention to the manager, but also bring income in for the restaurant. All in all — a win-win situation!

Specials:

Before asking the guests for their drink orders, tell them about any specials that day, which are not listed anywhere, and what the restaurant has 86'ed to eliminate disappointments. The reason is that some people will decide what to drink based on what they might want to eat. As the saying goes (if they are wine drinkers): "White wine with fish, red wine with meats."

Guests Wanting to Talk to One Another:

Sometimes guests are seated who will talk and talk from the moment they sit down. They may be businesspeople wanting to get their business discussion out of the way before enjoying a meal (or through the entire meal), or people who have not seen one another for a long time and want to catch up. In either case, try not to interrupt them or hover over them, no matter how antsy you might be. But at the same time your guests should not be neglected either.

Here is what you can do to put your guests, and yourself, at ease: tell them about the specials, give them other vital information, and then take their drink orders. When you deliver their drinks, then tell them, "When you are ready to order, just close your menus. Until then I'll just watch your drinks." That way you have a great visual cue, can keep an eye on their drinks, and can watch for the closed menus. Many guests have told me that this is a wonderful idea. It will allow the guests to relax. You have acknowledged their need to talk, and they realize that you are still attentive.

Guests in a Hurry:

If your guests are in a hurry, they usually tell you, and then you can make suggestions on what dishes are fast to come out of the kitchen and what they may not want to order. It will all depend on their time frame. (See Step 5 under "Presenting the Check.")

Singles:

When a single person comes in and is seated, every minute he or she has to wait for your attention seems like five minutes to him or her. Greet him or her immediately, and, if that is not possible, have the host greet him or her and get him or her something to drink. Acknowledge him or her in one way or another.

These people come in, eat, and leave almost as if they are in a hurry. If possible, try to strike up a conversation with them after putting in their order. (See "Talking with Guests," in Chapter 6.) Some people really like it that you take the time to talk to them, while others will not. You just have to remember to read the people and be careful with the topic.

Double Seating:

It's important for hosts to try not to do this, but I know sometimes it is out of their control. People come in and sit down where they want to — host or no host. When this happens, there are a couple of things you can do to make sure that both tables still get the attention they need. Everything will depend on timing and/or rules the establishment has set up.

The guests should always be greeted — **always!** If you cannot get to them, you should at least tell them, "Hi, my name is ____, and I will be right with you." Try to have a host, a manager, or another server start them with drinks, if possible. This little part can help you to get back on track. Acknowledging the guests is a key to success and a good guest relations tool.

Here is a suggestion of how to handle things if you are by yourself because everyone else is busy:

Get Drink Order Table 1	Get Drink Order Table 2	Drop Drinks at Table 2	Drop Drinks at Table 1 Take Order	Go to Table 2 Take Order	Put Both Orders In

Go to the first table and take their drink orders, then go to the second table and do the same. Always greet them by saying your name, any "skit" (rehearsed information the restaurant supplied or that you created), and converse to help your guests not to feel rushed or neglected. Then serve the drinks; go to the second table, first saying, "I will be right back to take your order or answer any questions"; then go to the first table; put the drinks down and take their order; and go back to the second table and take their order. Then put both orders in. Essentially you treat both tables as one big party. If one or the other is not ready, then they can be treated separately.

Keep in mind, though, that if one party is larger than the other, the smaller party should be attended to first. You get the drink orders in, if possible, but acknowledge the larger party. How you will handle this depends on the situation.

Step 2: Beverages

Some establishments use napkins or coasters to put drinks on to keep condensation off the table or to prevent rings from forming on a table-cloth, and others use them not only for the above but also as a visual cue that tells other servers and managers that the guests have been greeted and are being taken care of, the most important part of service.

Suggestive Selling is when you try to help sell items by describing them using descriptive words. What you are doing is painting a picture of the items in your guests' mind and teasing their palates.

Upselling is when you try to sell items in addition to the normal menu items, that are just a little higher in price, but can add lots of flavor or make the guests' dining experience more pleasurable.

Here's where suggested selling and upselling come in. Try to always suggest a beverage or the guests just may end up asking for water, which does not cost anything and would not increase the check amount. I tend to say something like this: "Can I get you something to drink? We have Iced Tea, Coke/Pepsi products, lemonade or a full service bar." If you think that they might be interested in a bar beverage, continue by mentioning a few favorites or describe a drink such as a Tiramisu Martini with Baileys, chocolate, vanilla vodka, Kahlua, and white chocolate liqueur.

When serving bottled water, make sure you use a cold glass with no ice. In the guests' eyes, ice will dilute the pureness of the water. The water is usually served with a lemon or lime wedge.

To prevent a glass from sticking to a paper napkin, you can sprinkle a little salt on the napkin before placing the glass on it. This is a bartender's trick.

When you pick up the beer from the bar to serve and see that there is no foam on top and the glass does not look quite full, stir it vigorously with a straw. Just be careful not to overdo it, or the foam will spill over.

When carrying trays with wine glasses or other stemware, you could try to hold them down on the tray using your entire hand and putting the stems between your fingers. This will help to keep the glasses on the tray when you have to maneuver around people and tables.

When carrying only one or two glasses of white wine, make sure that you hold them by the stem. If you hold the glass itself, your hands will be warming up the wine, and you don't want white wine to get warm. Many people ask for a glass of ice so they can put an ice cube or two into their wine to get it nicely chilled.

You should never go behind the bar to order or pick up drinks. You are only allowed behind the bar when in training and being instructed in mixing drinks, or when you are told just to observe the bartender. The reason is that there is a cash drawer and the bartenders are responsible for the drawer amounts.

Hot drinks should always be served first and collected last from the kitchen. If you have to get hot and cold beverages, make sure that you collect the cold beverages before the hot ones to prevent hot items from getting too cold.

To prevent running back and forth for hot drinks like coffee, tea, hot chocolate, or any other hot beverage, you should warm the cup or glass first. If this is not done, the cold temperature of the glass will cool down the beverage to lukewarm, and the guest might return it so it can be warmed up again.

When two or more guests are ordering the same wine, think about offering a bottle of wine, unless the wine is only sold by the glass, which is usually the house brand. This shows the guests that you are looking after their best interests and trying to save them money, which they will hopefully spend on more food, or you.

When the restaurant runs out of iced tea or iced coffee, the quickest way to make it is to double brew them and then add equal amounts of ice. The ice will melt, quickly cooling down the drink, but at the same time the beverage will maintain its usual strength, satisfying the guests.

When putting ground coffee in a filter, you should wet the edges a little around the top and press it against the plastic holder. This keeps the paper in place and prevents grinds from falling into the coffee.

Checking ID:

When serving alcohol, it is important for you to check the guests' IDs to make sure that they are of legal age. When checking a guest's ID look not only at the date, but also at the address and the hologram. Make sure that the picture looks like the person in front of you, then flip the ID over and look for the user code — but if in doubt, ask a question like what year he or she was born in, what is his or her address, or what town does he or she live in. His or her answer should come immediately without stopping to think about it. Any server has to attend a training class in which he or she will be taught how to go about this. After completion of the class the server will get certified.

When you ask people for their IDs and they look at you funny or say "Really?" because they are way over 21, you can say: "I have to check people's IDs if they look younger than 30, and you, Sir/Madam, really do." It is also the law that, if you request a drink, you must be able to show proof that you are over 21. So, no matter what your age is, when you go out and want to order a drink, have your license or another ID with you.

Alternatives:

When guests order alcoholic drinks and you do not have the specific one they are asking for, you should always come up with an alternative when needed. For instance, if the establishment is out of or does not carry Ketel One Vodka, you would say: "I am sorry, we do not have Ketel One, but may I suggest Absolut or Gray Goose?" or "Is there another brand you might care for?" If a guest asks for a certain brand and you do not know if the restaurant carries it, you can ask your guest for others like it, and then ask the bartender which ones they have. This happens a lot with brandy or scotch.

It is always good to know the top three brands in each liquor category to be able to respond quickly and more professionally.

Opening Wine Bottles:

This is a skill every server and especially the bartender should master. There are a couple of different ways of doing it, but I find that the easiest way is to do it as described below. You should just check with the establishment to see if they agree with this method.

First, make sure that the wine, if not red, has been chilled. Here are two ways to keep it cold; both are effective:

1. A wine chiller comes from a refrigerator and is usually a metal or marble container which is placed on the table.

2. A bucket which is filled half with ice and enough water to allow room for the bottle. The bucket sits next to the table on its own stand.

Red wine does not get chilled before serving.

Second, follow this procedure for serving it:

1. Place an empty glass in front of each person who will be drinking wine. Check to make sure there are no lipstick or water spots on the glasses before bringing them to the table.

2. Show the bottle to the person (the host) who ordered it so he or she can confirm that it is what the party ordered, and be sure that the label is always in the host's view.

3. Never put the bottle on the table when opening it. Hold the bottle in one hand and take out the wine opener, preferably the two-step opener, since that is the easiest to use and the one I will be describing.

4. Open the knife and start cutting. I tend to go straight up the foil from the bottom to the top. Even if the foil does not come off right away, there will be a wide gap so the rest of the foil can be pulled off. This is not the professional way, but it is quick and

easy. Cutting around the lip of the bottle is a more professional way, but, unless done properly, that procedure results in having many pieces and having to turn the bottle with the label around.

5. Once the foil is removed, put the knife away, put the tip of the corkscrew in the middle of the cork, and twist it downward until the last screw or spiral is visible.

6. With one hand hold the bottle and with the thumb push against the notched **middle** lever so that the first corner snaps into the lip of the bottle.

7. Pull up the handle with the other hand, which will pull the cork halfway out.

8. Release the first notch of the lever by pushing down the handle placing the notched **end** lever on the bottle rim, holding it with the thumb.

9. Pull up the handle, and the cork will come out completely.

10. Pour a little amount of the wine into the host's glass for him or her to try.

11. When approved, fill the ladies' glasses first (from the oldest to the youngest), then the glasses of the gentlemen in the party (from the oldest to the youngest) — filling the host's glass last, no matter if it is a man or a woman.

12. When filling the glasses, never lift a glass from the table. Make your way around the table, and if the guests are seated in a booth, reach over the center of the table, saying "Excuse me," if needed.

13. A wine bottle holds approximately four glasses. So, depending on the number of people, use your judgment to make sure that everyone gets some. If there is plenty, fill the glasses only halfway and put the remainder in the bucket or on the table.

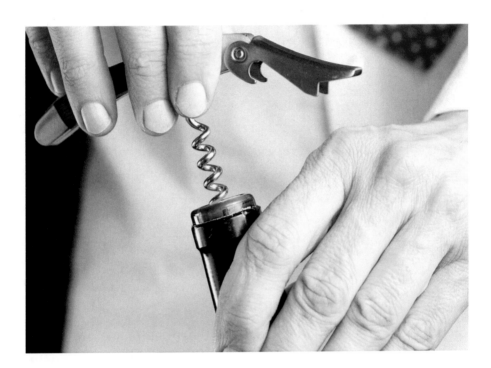

Step 3: Taking Orders

All servers should follow the procedures set by the establishment. If the restaurant offers free bread, you should try not to bring the bread out before you had the chance to take your guest's appetizer or food order. You would want your guests to remain hungry, so that there is a better chance of them ordering appetizers before their meal. The more the guests order, the higher the bill will be, and the more tips you may receive. Many servers bring bread with the drinks to save themselves some extra steps, yet they run the risk that the guests will fill up on bread before they are ready to order. But if you really need to save steps, then by all means bring out the bread with the drinks.

When doing suggestive selling, instead of just asking if they would like an appetizer or telling them what the specials are, describe them: "Would you like mushrooms stuffed with pork, herbs, and spices?", or "Would you like the salmon with a lemon butter sauce and garlic mashed potatoes?" Your establishment can help you here.

Make the guests aware when an item comes with a sauce. People don't always read the menu thoroughly and take in the details. If a guest is not sure if she/he wants the sauce, you, if allowed by the establishment, may be able to put it on the side so your guest can still enjoy the meal, and maybe even try a sauce that may be new to him or her.

Repeat the order as you take it, because, when the restaurant is busy, the noise level is higher — or there may be items on the menu that sound alike, and you may not hear correctly. Hearing one thing and ordering another from the kitchen spells trouble. Not only is the guest dissatisfied but so is management. Repeating what someone orders has saved me many times with the kitchen because they did not have to fix any mistakes, which, of course, would throw off their rhythm. Getting an order right the first time also saves the server a lot of running back and forth.

Writing all the orders down makes the guests feel more comfortable and cuts down on any mistakes. Trying to impress the guests with one's memory does not work anymore. It only makes the guests worry and wonder if their food is going to come out of the kitchen right or wrong. You don't want them feeling stressed about their meal half of the time when they should be relaxing and enjoying the evening or afternoon.

Position Points:

These are points or seat numbers used to determine how food will be placed on the table. It is **important** for you to know how to number your seats in the same way. The main reason is that, if you are unable to serve the food to the table assigned to you, someone else is able to and will **not** have to "auction off" the ordered menu items.

Another reason for numbering seats is for you to keep track of who ordered what, which includes meals, drinks, and dessert. If at the end of the meal someone in the party asks for separate checks, that's not a problem when you have everything organized on paper. Most POS systems are setup to ask what position seat number this item is going to and even have a separate button that says "separate by seat" to help assist you.

A point of sale (POS) system is a system by which a restaurant sells items. It usually consists of a computer, cash register, and debit or credit card reader.

In most places the numbering works like this: With your back toward the bar, the front door, or to the kitchen, whichever management prefers, Position One always starts with the first seat to the left of the server's position, and then continues clockwise around the table.

The illustration below shows a restaurant layout where the servers have their backs toward the kitchen, depending on the location of the table:

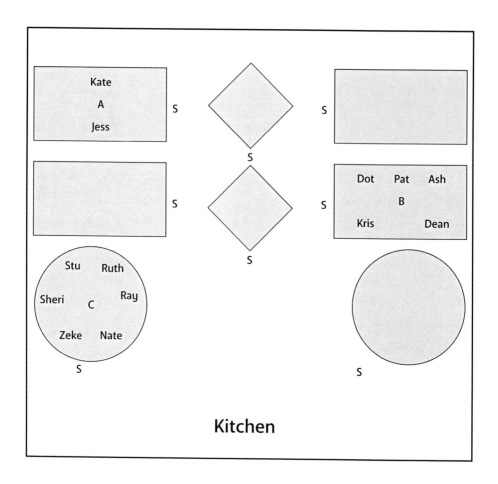

If the server's back is toward the kitchen and a guest is right in front as shown in Table C, he or she should step to the left between two guests. Position 1 starts with Zeke.

Some restaurants use all seat numbers, even if no one is sitting in that position. For example: in Table A, Jess is seat 1 and Kate seat 4; and in Table B, Dot is seat 1, Pat seat 2, Ash seat 3, Dean seat 4, and Kris seat 6. In other restaurants, they just go in order around the tables. For example: Jess is seat 1 and Kate is seat 2 — and at Table B Dot is seat 1, Pat seat 2, Ash seat 3, Dean seat 4, and Kris seat 5. The latter system is so much easier and more common. Check with the trainer or manager to find out which way they want it to be done and where Position One would start.

Extras and Changes:

Do not make any changes to any items without consent from the manager. For instance, if ice cream does not come with whipped cream, do not add any; and if the bread doesn't come with oil and Parmesan cheese, do not add it. All extra things added affect the bottom line of the establishment. If too many servers add them for free, the costs of operating the restaurant go up, the company will have to raise their prices, and then fewer guests may come in. The same goes when it comes to swapping vegetables. If the main meal comes with broccoli and the guest wants asparagus, it may be done (know the menu and what's allowed), but might be at an added cost to the guest. Mixed vegetables may or may not be separated. Make sure that your guests know if there is an up-charge.

This is just what happened when I was working in a family restaurant. One of the servers decided to not only serve the traditional bread and butter, but also to bring out oil and Parmesan cheese. The server took the oil that was to be used to make salad dressings and the cheese from containers that were set aside for pasta dishes.

These same guests used to come into the restaurant once a week and, of course, always asked for the extras they had received before. Others in the restaurant noticed and started asking for the same, and, of course, they told their friends and family. The result: the company had to purchase much bigger amounts of cheese and oil and raise their prices.

Another server's action also affects you, because the next time the guests visit they will ask for those items again and, if you say that the restaurant doesn't offer those extras, the guest will complain that they got the items the last time, which makes you look bad because you were not aware of what the other server was doing. You might think that you are giving your guests great service when you offer something that is not on the menu or give them extras, but this "great service" can soon snowball out of control.

Placing Orders With the Kitchen:

When the restaurant becomes very busy, things can start to go wrong. It is important to keep organized to minimize any problems that can occur. Sometimes guests will order an appetizer at the same time they order their main meal. When you are taking the orders at several tables, you may not remember all the details.

You would want the appetizers, and then salads and/or soups to come out of the kitchen before the entrees. Here is the trick I use: when I have multiple orders on one sheet in my note book (Figure A) I put a check mark on the side of the item when I have submitted the order to the kitchen (Figure B).

Table # & # Guests	P Pt	Beverage	Prep Items Key: Ketchup / Sugar Caddy / Stk Sauce / Mustard / Crushed Red Pepper / Dressing	Dessert
			MISSION *To Create An Environment Where Absolute Guest Satisfaction Is Our Highest Priority.*	
6∅	1	COFFEE	App / Entrée CALAMARI CK ALFREDO Modification/Prep	X
	2	ICED TEA	App / Entrée HAMBURGER M FF Modification/Prep	
	3	ICED TEA	App / Entrée KID'S PASTA Modification/Prep NO CHZ	
7∅	1	WATER	App / Entrée FILET M Modification/Prep	✓
	2	WATER	App / Entrée CK CAESAR Modification/Prep NO CROUTONS	
5∅	1	ICED TEA	App / Entrée FRIED CHZ HAMBURGER M FF Modification/Prep	✓
	2	WATER	App / Entrée CLUB FF Modification/Prep	

Figure A

5∅	1	ICED TEA	App / Entrée FRIED CHZ HAMBURGER M FF Modification/Prep	✓
	2	WATER	App / Entrée CLUB FF Modification/Prep	

Figure B

Once the appetizers, salads, or soups are out, I put a line through the check mark and then the main dishes can be ordered and checked off. (Figure C)

Table # & # Guests	P Pt	Beverage	Prep Items Key: Ketchup / Sugar Caddy / Stk Sauce / Mustard / Crushed Red Pepper / Dressing		Dessert
6Ø	1	COFFEE	App / Entrée CALAMARI CK ALFREDO .... Modification/Prep		X
	2	ICED TEA	App / Entrée HAMBURGER M FF .... Modification/Prep		
	3	ICED TEA	App / Entrée KID'S PASTA .... Modification/Prep NO CHZ		✓

Figure C

Once I have served all the items at the tables, I draw a single line through the entire list. (Figure D)

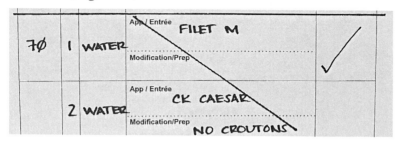

| 7Ø | 1 | WATER | App / Entrée   FILET M   .... Modification/Prep | | ✓ |
| | 2 | WATER | App / Entrée   CK CAESAR   .... Modification/Prep NO CROUTONS | | |

Figure D

When the guests are done eating and have received their check, I draw another line through the list of items, making an X. With multiple orders from different tables entered on one paper, I know what I sent to the kitchen without having to check the computer, which sometimes is hard to get to.

Some computers allow you to enter the entire order without sending it all to the kitchen. For instance: after the appetizer order has been sent to the kitchen, the entree can be put in, but "on hold." This system of check marks manually helps remind you of what has been sent and what still needs to be sent to the kitchen. Once the appetizers are out, you just have to hit the "send" button instead of entering it all on the computer.

When you are done entering the items on the computer, make sure you review what you entered and correct any mistakes you may have made before you hit the "send" button. I once entered a large order, and when I reviewed it I noticed an item I did not want to order. I deleted the item, checked my book to see what the guests had ordered, and noticed that I had mistakenly punched (with my fat fingers) the item just below the one the guests wanted. By reviewing my entries, I prevented the kitchen from preparing the wrong item and my guests from having to wait for the correct item to be made. For me, not to have to involve a manager was priceless.

Once the guests have placed their orders and you have submitted them to the kitchen, make idle talk to take your guests' mind off the waiting time until the food comes out of the kitchen, especially when the kitchen is taking longer to get the food out, which helps make that connection.

Step 4: Serving and Maintenance

When serving warm bread try not to serve rock-hard, cold butter with it. Trying to spread hard butter on soft bread would just rip it apart. And it's a pain to have to wait until the butter softens enough on the warm bread so it can be spread. Keeping the butter on ice is the best way to serve it cold, but not too hard.

When a guest has ordered a soda or other refillable drink, has not yet received his or her meal, and has already drunk half of the contents, serve him or her a new one automatically. If the party is eating and one of the guests has drunk half of his or her drink, ask if he or she wants the glass refilled. This shows attention to detail and makes sure that your guest is satisfied. If fresh drinks must be purchased again, then, of course, you should always ask.

When a glass is empty, you can either refill it or take it away. Always remove an empty glass when you bring another full one — don't leave it on the table. If the guest does not want it to be refilled and it is empty, remove it completely.

Once the order is sent to the kitchen, you want to anticipate any needs the guest may have. Bring extra plates for any food items the guests want to share. When serving appetizers make sure that your guests have small bread plates, or something similar, to put the food on, if they are not already part of the table setup.

Before serving the next courses, the tables should be pre-bussed and the next course utensils, if needed, placed on the table. For instance: When the guests are done with the appetizers, remove the plates, and, if they ordered soup, bring a soup spoon, unless it is already placed with the bowl or cup. If they ordered a steak and a steak knife is not already placed on the table with the other silverware, put one out before the meal arrives. These are little details guests may not be aware of, but will definitely notice if they don't have something they need later.

When a restaurant uses large trays to put food on and does not use tray stands in the kitchen, then the trays become very hot underneath from heat lamps. My trick to keep the food hot and the tray cooler, and easier to carry, is to put a thick knife, or anything similar, under the tray. This will lift the tray off the table or counter and the air can flow underneath thereby keeping the tray cooler.

Before taking any food from the kitchen, look it over to make sure that everything they ordered is correct and that the food looks appealing (not burned or dried out, e.g., pasta). If anything looks wrong or not appealing, have it fixed. This is difficult to do when there are food runners or other servers helping you to run food, but even then everyone should be doing it. Making sure that things go out correctly can stop a lot of unnecessary complaints and can show the guests that you are listening to them.

Be careful to place tray stands out of the way of traffic and not where guests and other servers may walk. This will help not only the flow of the restaurant, but also it will prevent someone from knocking into the stand and dumping food on the floor.

When the plates are hot, warn the guests so they do not reach for the plate and try to take it, which is a natural reaction. If they do, you have to be ready to pull it back before they touch it. Kids' plates should **never** be hot. (And darn, if I do not see this all the time!) Make sure to switch a hot plate with one that can be touched.

When serving, make sure to put the main course in front of the guest.

Serve children first, then the oldest lady in the party to the youngest, then the men, from the oldest to the youngest. Try to serve from the left and take empty plates from the right.

If ramekins are put directly on the plates, make sure that the ramekin is placed furthest away from the guest. Ramekins usually contain some sort of sauce or side item. So, if it is not on the main dish plate, you have to make sure that a small plate is placed under it and you may want to place a spoon with it. It makes it a lot easier for a guest to be able to use the right amount of the item instead of pouring or dumping it.

Whenever you do bring anything to the table that was not included originally — like extra sauce, straws, lemons, etc. — take care either to place those items on a clean plate or napkin or to wrap them in something clean.

After you serve the food and ask if there is anything else the guests might need, and they say "Nothing," you can make some suggestions of items the guests may not have thought about. That can save you from having to make trips back and forth to the table. If the guests call for something else later and you are tied up at another table, tell them, "OK, I'll get that in a moment," and finish what you were doing. Then go and get the item. (See "Saving Steps.")

But even when you are busy with other tables, you should always check back after two minutes or two bites and make sure your guests are enjoying their meal. When doing so, be more specific when asking questions. Instead of saying "How is everything?" you could ask, "Is your steak cooked the way you like it?" or "Do you like the garlic butter on your salmon?" Being specific gives the guest a feeling of importance and an opportunity to state any negative feelings. If the meat is not cooked properly and the guests have to wait for you to come back, and even longer for the kitchen to prepare a new steak, they may have a negative reaction toward you and the restaurant.

Whenever you want to remove a plate ask, "May I take your plate?" This is a nice way of asking if they have finished. Some guests want their plates taken away the minute they are done; others want to wait until everyone is done eating, so the slower eaters do not feel rushed. The only way to find out is to ask. You should check with the establishment to see if there is a preference about handling this task.

Removing most of the dishes unclutters the table, makes the guests feel more comfortable, and makes it faster and easier to clean up after the guests are gone. Forks and spoons may be replaced if the guests order dessert or coffee. After the guests are finished with dessert, the only things left on the table should be their drinks.

Packing Up Food:

When you pack up the leftover food, use gloves, paper, or utensils — but never let your fingers touch it. If you wrap the food up at the table, bring boxes and bags of different sizes, and when the tables are too small to work on, use a tray with a stand, if the establishment has them.

When dumping food into a box, the food does not always look very pretty. Try to scoop it as well as you can and, if possible, ask the guest for assistance. The guests normally do not have a problem with that. Salads have the tendency to fall all over the place due to very small pieces. My trick with packing large salads is to put the box over the salad, as long as the salad fits the size of the box, and flip it over.

One trick I use is to put a knife under the sandwich or burger and a fork on top to lift them into the box.

I received a comment saying: "Oh, I see, you have done this many times before!" People loved to see me do it.

For other food items you could use a fork, knife or a spoon to slide it off the plate and into a to-go box. You can do this either right at the table or in the kitchen — whatever the guest prefers or the establishment allows.

Step 5: Desserts and Payment

The time to ask if the guests would like to order desserts is when they are three-quarters through their meal. You can suggest one or two different desserts, saying, "Are you saving room for some delicious homemade cheesecake or fudge brownie?" or "Make sure you have some room for …" or "Don't forget to save room for …" If they seem interested you can start describing one such as "a warmed-up double fudge brownie with ice-cream and topped with chocolate sauce?" or mention some more items. For upselling try to offer special dessert toppings.

If they are too full for dessert, a smart thing to do is to suggest a dessert to go. That way you increase the check amount and also flip the table at the same time.

Presenting the Check:

Make sure you review the check before dropping it. This will ensure that you give the right check to the right person.

When guests come in just to have a leisurely meal with friends, or business people for an informal meeting, like at lunchtime, you can drop the check on the table after asking if they would like dessert. When they come in and are in a hurry, and guests will usually let you know that, it is important that you ask them if they would like any dessert either here or to go. If the answer is "Yes," you can drop the check when you bring the dessert, and if the answer is "No," you can drop the check when you bring the entree.

This not only acknowledges their time frame but also allows them to relax because they can pay for the meal right away when it is delivered and not have to wait for you to bring them the check later.

Some establishments now have a phone application which allows for the guests to pay using their phone. I personally do not like this because it leaves too much control in the hands of the guests. They can decide when to close the bill. What happens when they forget to do it? Some establishments close the bill after a certain amount of time, but, of course, without adding a tip.

Before taking any payment make sure that the guests saw the bill and had a chance to check it over. When it's time to bring the check, you may want to stand the book up, not lay it down flat on the table, because when the guests handle it they tend to put the book flat on the table, and then you can see that they might be ready to pay.

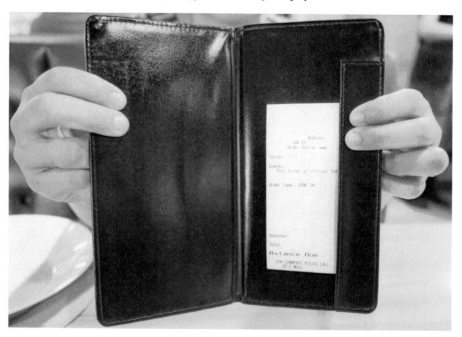

You can drop the check with these words: "I'll put this here for your convenience, but if you need anything else, just let me know."

Dropping the check, especially at dinner, can sometimes become tricky when one of the guests insists that he or she wants to pay. Always give the check to the first person who asks for it. I find that most of the servers tend to do this.

I literally had one gentleman guest come into the kitchen and thrust his credit card at me before they even ordered drinks, and a lady poke at my leg with her credit card under the table. Oh, well! At least I knew whom to give the check to.

Accepting Payment:

When you think that the guests are finished looking over the bill and put down the checkbook, pick it up right away.

There are four things that will usually happen:

1. If you do not see any kind of payment in the checkbook, you could say: "I'll be right back with this." This will allow the guest to say: "I did not do it yet," or "I don't need anything back," or "OK."

2. If you see cash, you can say that you will be back with the change. Then the guest may say: "No, you keep it," or "OK, thanks." Then, when giving the change back to them, you should try to give them enough smaller bills so they can leave a 20-25 percent tip. Always carry enough smaller bills in your cash bank. Most servers carry two dollars in coins, four five-dollar bills, one ten-dollar bill, and at least ten one-dollar bills. When you count the change back to the guest you acknowledge the amounts at the same time, and the guest cannot come back later claiming that he or she did not receive the correct change.

3. If you see a credit card, then "I'll be right back with this" applies. If two credit cards are placed in the checkbook, usually the guests want the check split evenly. If in doubt, ask.

4. When the guest puts down his or her credit card and some cash, never assume that the extra cash is your tip. Always ask the guest what you should do with it. "Would you like me to take the cash amount off the bill before I run the credit card?" Some people will say "Yes" because others in the party may have given them cash, and the rest goes on the credit card. Others may say that it is the tip.

When taking the credit card, look carefully at it to be sure it is not a debit card. Some credit cards are actually debit cards. If it is a debit card it will say "Debit" on the bottom of the right-hand corner. If you process the card as a credit card and it is not, it can have dire consequences for the guest if anything goes wrong.

Here is what may happen: When a credit or debit card is run, an Authorization Code is issued, the money in the guest's checking account is put on hold, and is not released until the bank processes it for payment. If you make a mistake and have to run the card again, and if the Authorization Code is not used again, that amount will also be put on hold and handled by the bank just as the first amount. Meanwhile, the guest cannot use any money that is on hold. And if there is a dispute, it can take who knows how long. The manager should know to use the same Authorization Code and enter the correct amount. But this takes a lot of time, so try to be careful when processing a credit or debit card. This fix will not happen until the restaurant compiles all the credit card charges, which is usually at the end of the work day. In some cases gift cards can cause the same problem if you make a mistake when entering them into the system. Some entries can be corrected at a later date; some cannot be corrected at all.

Most establishments are now forcing servers to enter the three digit CCV/CCD code number from the back of the credit or debit card, and even if you don't enter the code, always check it to see if the guest wrote his or her name, "See ID," "Check ID," or "See Photo" on it. Except for the name, if you see any one of those phrases, you should act on it when you go back to the table. People write those things on their cards to protect themselves from fraud. They really appreciate it when a server pays attention to their request (and maybe leave a better tip). I was once given a 25 percent tip just for asking.

It is a good idea to put the guests' credit card in front of the credit card slip when bringing it back for them to sign.

If they should forget it, you have to run after them and try to catch them before they get to their car.

If they paid by credit card, make sure that you get back before they leave to make sure that the total is correct and that the credit card slip is signed. These can be corrected as long as the guests are still there. If the amount is wrong and the guests are no longer there, how to handle it would depend on the practices of the establishment. My advice is: as long as you can clearly read the total on the bill, not the final total, and the amount of the tip, you can use that information to feed into the computer.

Some restaurants will not give the server the tip if there is no signature, because the guest could claim that they never ate in the restaurant. Of course, the restaurant would not get paid either if they do that. This is where the CCV/CCD code comes in handy.

Also, it happens quite often that people take the signed copy leaving the blank one on the table, or they take both copies. I have caught people before they got into their cars and retrieved the receipt from them. If you do not act right away, they may be long gone. Some establishments might eventually write the server up for it when it happens.

When picking up the signed credit card slip, or even cash, make sure to say something like: "Thank you very much, and have a wonderful day," "Thank you, I hope to see you in the future," or "Thank you, I hope to see you again." You do not have to be afraid to pick up the slip right away. Generally, people do not care and do not see it as being money hungry.

If a credit card is ever left behind, give it to the manager, so he can put it in a safe place. Then, when the owner comes back for it, the manager can ask him or her for proper ID before handing it over.

Conclusion

As a server, you learn more about the importance of teamwork, the proper ways of doing the job, things you should be aware of, and what you can do in each "step of service" that can benefit you and your guest. You also learn the reasons to know and understand the menu items, the tools of the trade, the importance of continued training, and how to solve problems or preventing them from occurring in the first place. The last bit of knowledge to gain, besides going on salary like a manager, is the bartender position.

Chapter 8

Bartenders

Communication with servers

One of a bartender's responsibilities is to make sure that guests who only drink at the bar are of age by checking their IDs as mentioned under Chapter 7, Step 2.

A bartender not only serves guests at the bar but also supplies alcoholic drinks to the waitstaff serving guests in the dining room.

If you notice that the same server repeatedly gets the same kind of drink, you should ask the server if those drinks are for the same guest. This communication between you and the server is crucial, because both of you can try to prevent a guest from becoming intoxicated.

Logbooks

It is important to keep a logbook at the bar. It is a way to keep track of any event that is happening in the bar that you might want to recall later or tell other bartenders or managers about.

The logbook should have entries about the following:

- When a guest has been cut off
- When a cab had to be called
- When someone became violent
- When someone verbally abused someone
- When someone walks in already intoxicated

It can be very beneficial in any investigation if you can collect information such as names of the offenders, description of their looks, what they were wearing, anything they said or did, etc. — and write all of the details down while they are still fresh in your mind. (See the section on logbooks in Chapter 9.)

The logbook can also be used to pass information from one bartender to the next. For instance, "Couldn't stock because the merchandise did not come in," "We are out of Stoli," messages guests may want to leave for a certain bartender, just a note telling someone what has been done or what has not, or how great he or she is.

Substitutions

Do not substitute one alcohol for another unless you ask the guest first. I once went with a friend to have a drink, and she had told the bartender that she wanted Midori in her drink. When she tasted it, she knew right off that it did not contain Midori but melon instead. She sent the drink back and ordered a totally different drink, and made sure this time that the bartender used the ingredients she requested. An incident like this caused two negative things: 1) the bartender had an angry and dissatisfied guest, and 2) good drink ingredients were wasted because the drink had to be thrown away. Again — try to avoid problems.

Cash drawer

If the establishment uses only one drawer to be used by multiple bartenders, any shortages or surpluses — as well as tips, if they are put in — must be shared by all bartenders equally. The drawer normally contains a set amount of cash (e.g., $300.00) that has to be verified by you before your shift begins. Once you agree, the drawer is placed in the register and becomes your responsibility while you are working the shift. It is important to be able to count quickly. If there are two bartenders on duty and handling money is not your strong area, I suggest you do the service bar. If the establishment uses two drawers, then each bartender is assigned to one and responsible for the amount of cash in it. In this case, neither bartender should have access to the other drawer. It is your responsibility to make sure that servers do not go behind the bar so you have better control over your cash drawers.

Opening the bar

Before the bar can open for business you should make sure that:

a) Countertops, bar stools, and floors are clean. The bar stools should be arranged either all facing the bar, or are all on the same angle.

b) The bar is set up with all of the normal tools, and, for added guest hospitality, things like newspapers, reading glasses, napkins, bar mats, etc. If bar mats show logos or advertisements of any sort on them, they should always face the guests.

c) Speed racks are arranged in a way all bartenders agree upon for ease of use.

d) Glasses are completely stocked, including cold beer and martini glasses. Any glasses hanging from racks should be clean, spotless, and have no lipstick residue or spots on them. They should also be checked for any chips, because these glasses are usually thinner than regular water glasses.

e) Bottles are arranged in groups — vodka, gin, etc. together — and backup bottles of house wine are opened for faster service. Each bottle should have a designated spot so that any bartender can easily feel for a bottle he or she needs without looking around to pick the correct one — for instance, the third bottle from the left bottom row is bar vodka. It will make it that much more entertaining for the guests when they watch the bartender grabbing a bottle and mixing the drinks while he or she never takes his or her eyes off them.

f) The sinks are ready for cleaning glasses, blenders, etc.

g) There is sufficient ice.

h) Cut fruit is ready to use.

i) There may be many other tasks to be performed based on the establishment's needs.

The entire bar should always look inviting to the guests. Some establishments put menus and silverware on the counter to encourage people to order food, not just drinks.

Cleanliness is a must! When, for instance, you use a utensil or a machine like a blender, you have to make sure that they are washed immediately after use so they will be ready for the next drink that you have to prepare.

To be a good bartender you have to acquire a great deal of knowledge. It takes some time, but once the skills are obtained you will be faster and more efficient. For instance, you have to know terminologies, beer and wine brands, where all the bottles are, what kind of glasses to use for what drinks, how to measure or count liquor for drinks, how much fruit needs to be cut based on the volume of guests, what fruit goes with what drinks, how many wine bottles to open and how many bottles to stock, how to use the equipment, and so on.

Getting to know people is part of inducing guests to come back and become "regulars." Every bar has steady guests. It means that the guests enjoy the company of the bartender or other patrons who frequently come in. You can help promote this practice by introducing them to each other at the bar. You play a major role in the guests having an enjoyable time.

I once tended a horseshoe bar serving six people at the same time. The fun part was that they all came from a different state and had come to New Hampshire for the foliage season. Through me, everybody got engaged in the same conversation. They all insisted that their state was better than the others. After listening to them argue for about five minutes, I piped in and said: "You are all wrong. New Hampshire is the best."

They all agreed with me and had a good laugh. Some of the same guests came back the following year. They remembered me and the fun they had.

Bartending can be fun and has a very special social aspect. People tend to go to a bar when they are alone, when they just like to chat with someone, or both. As I once heard: "If you want to feel better about your own problems, become a bartender and listen to everyone's problems; they are usually worse."

While all positions — host, server, and bartender — present many opportunities for you to provide good service and have a fulfilling occupation, maybe you want to move on to a different role as a manager. By getting to this point in the book, you've learned a lot about the FOH jobs. It's time to move on to the next and last part — management.

Part Four

Managers

Chapter 9

General Information

Introduction

A manager's responsibilities encompass every skill needed for the successful operation of an establishment. A manager has to be a leader, a diplomat, a communication expert to handle personnel and guest issues, a counselor, a problem solver, a person who knows how to do marketing, a great listener with a thorough dose of understanding, and much more.

Knowledge a manager would want to attain should include: how to control labor costs, food and liquor costs, inventory costs, hiring, and more. If the company does not have a human resource person, the manager also has to know firing practices, the state labor laws, immigration law, Americans With Disabilities Act, etc. A manager needs to know by whom and in what someone needs to be certified — whatever the state law requires. For example, OSHA, BASSET, SERVE-SAFE, CPR, or any other organization or certification. I mention this because, unfortunately, many managers do not have this information.

I strongly suggest that anybody, before he or she becomes a manager, works in each restaurant position he or she may become in charge of. That may include: dishland, host, bar, server, expo, and even cook. A manager will earn more respect from the staff if he or she can jump into each position, when needed. He or she will also uphold the term "hospitality" and increase guest satisfaction when he or she is able to help the staff when they desperately need it.

Basic actions managers should take, which most managers do not:

a) Set rules and make sure that they are **enforced** by all managers.

b) Listen and try to understand, or in case of conflicts, don't just say, "That is the way it is done." Explain why and teach.

c) Follow through on what has been said.

d) Perform the required office tasks: inventory, costs, scheduling (when the restaurant is **not busy.**)

e) Follow the suggestions in this book and become a great leader and boss!

The things mentioned in this section are not everything a manager needs to know but are all things that are overlooked or not practiced — the missing pieces that most establishments do not have or understand.

Availability

During peak hours, you have to be available at all times to deal with any problem or issues that may arise. The faster a problem can be resolved, the better the atmosphere will be in the restaurant for the staff and the guests.

If you happen to be tied up, for instance, in doing an interview, doing office work, or taking inventory, you would have to make sure that another manager is on the floor and available to solve a problem, so a server does not waste time running around locating one. If that is not possible, the staff should know where they can find you, so they can ask you what to do in any situation. Too many times a server wastes precious time, and the guests are becoming frustrated because they have to wait for the server to track down a manager.

Cash registers

Make sure that the cash registers and bar drawers are set up to hold mostly small bills. The drawers should also contain a couple of $20 bills to be used when guests bring in $100 bills to pay for a $20 charge. This happens more often than you think. It's embarrassing when a server has to pay back $80 in ones and fives.

Checking grounds

A very important job you would want to do, or have someone else do, is to check the grounds around the building and parking lot for discarded cigarette butts and any other kind of garbage. This is often overlooked, but when guests see dirt and litter outside they may think that, if the outside is trashy, the inside may be just as bad. Besides, who really wants to see garbage when entering a place to eat? Yuck!

Checkout

Every restaurant I have worked in had a server called a "shift leader," or "head server." These servers would always "check out" everyone else who had been working to make sure that all the side work was done and they were the last ones to leave. In order for this to work effectively, you **must** then "check out" the shift-leader. If this is not done, the staff has a tendency not to complete their work.

Certifications

In most states staff members must be certified in liquor serving and food safety. State programs can be taken online, in-house as a group, or at a certain location. They may be listed under different names such as TIPS, BASSET or OSHA. These certificates become part of the employee file and should be maintained and updated.

Certifications are often overlooked but are necessary for the establishment as well as the person completing a training program. The police department, for instance, needs people who serve alcohol to be certified. It is the law in most states, if not all of them. This would include servers and bartenders. Any restaurant manager or another key employee can be certified to teach a course to others. If no one is available, an employee must sign up for a class online, at the local police department, or a manager can get a teacher and hold the class at the restaurant.

In either case, a new person, after training, who does not possess a certificate needed to do the job, must get one before they start to work. It is the law. Knowledge in this area can prevent problems and save the company from any potential lawsuits.

The same goes for a certificate an employee receives after being trained in safe food handling. A course like that would help to prevent food contamination and the possibility of guests becoming ill. In addition to the above-mentioned state programs, a program can also be found on video and can be done on a TV in the office, or on a computer. Again, this has to be done before employees serve guests. It is the law.

A certificate in CPR is not required, but a course in CPR would be beneficial for the restaurant and the individual. A person who knows CPR can help anyone who should be unfortunate enough to suffer a choking incidence or a heart attack. Yes, I have witnessed a heart attack, and also assisted an elderly man when he was choking. It can and does happen occasionally in a restaurant. Your local American Heart Association conducts courses, and fees are very low or there are none at all if done in a group setting.

Getting people certified is one thing, following what they learned is another. You must know what was taught, back it up, and make sure that all standards are being followed. If you do not follow through, courses become obsolete, the restaurant is put into peril, and no respect will be shown to you.

Comment cards

If an establishment uses comment cards, they are either dropped off by the guests at the host stand, put into a comment box, or given to you. This is a great way to help determine if there are any areas which need to be looked into, any problems that need to be addressed, or even to pass on any thank yous to the staff. Many people do not want to fill them out if there was a problem because they do not want to make a big deal out of it, so placing a comment box close to the exit might help, but the servers have to make sure to tell them this. It can coax people into dropping one in right before they exit.

Computer setup

When setting up a computer system, or changing an existing one, take care that items are easy to find or change. When looking at the menu you can decide what may go with an item, what could be modified, and in what order these selections should appear. The more buttons that can be pushed by a server, bartender, or a take-out person, the faster the person can operate.

There should always be a memo, special instructions button, or "See Server" button which can be pushed for things that may not be popular, hard to communicate, or to communicate better, but having a button for ingredients and such will help expedite the process.

I worked for a place that had an extra button for sauces, dressings, and food preparation. Not every sauce appeared under "sauce," some were under "food preparation," and some dressings were under "sauce." Very confusing and time consuming for a server to hunt for the right item.

Giving staff members the chance to give their input will help improve or shape the way the system is laid out. They know which buttons may be needed or which can be deleted, and what screen should come up first or second. Since the staff works with the system continuously, they will know even more than you. For instance: On the last screen putting instructions first such as SOS, extra, No, etc., and then the food items on the same screen, will make it quicker for the server to locate them. Speed is essential when the place is busy. See diagram below.

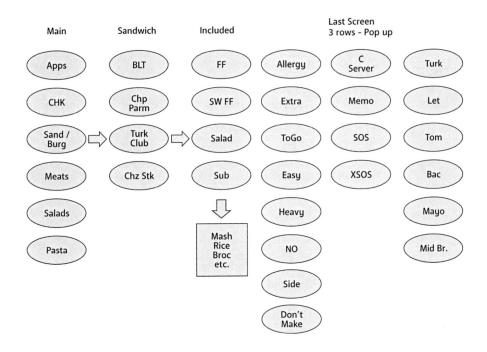

1st Screen — Main List: Category of food items.

2nd Screen — List of Items in That Category: Sandwiches.

3rd Screen — List of What Is Included: If a salad is picked, dressings should follow. If sub is picked, then all sub items are listed.

Last Screen — Lists of Options and Ingredients.

We all know that the system needs to be updated periodically during the day. But try to do these updates before shifts, or between shifts, if possible. It is annoying for a server when the system is offline and they are trying to ring in an order, run a credit card, or print a check.

Costs

Labor:

When it comes to FOH labor costs you need to be able to put structure into your efforts to help the business save money, and more so for BOH, which is on an hourly rate. For instance: If there are currently 15 people working on the floor and the rush is dying down, the servers can leave the floor and gradually go down to closers.

If you are not comfortable with removing servers from the floor, you can tell them that they will not be seated with new guests, and that they should go and do their side work, but at the same time to check on their remaining guests every two to three minutes. But if the business picks up again, they would be required to go back on the floor. That way they cannot complain about the decision you are making. If they are not needed by the time they have completed their side work, all guests are gone, no new guests have arrived, and they are ready to leave, then they should be free to go.

It is also very important to know the staff's abilities, and how many tables they can serve at the same time and still give excellent service without a guest becoming dissatisfied. This will give you the opportunity to cut back on the number of servers needed to schedule for the shift and thereby saving labor costs and allowing staff to earn good money. (More under "Scheduling.") The goal here is to keep the staff busy, happy, and earning money — and for you to feel comfortable.

Inventory, Food, and Liquor Costs:

Among other things, for the company to be able to calculate their income and losses, the FOH and BOH must keep accurate inventory on food, liquor, and dry storage items.

As the FOH manager you must record not only the purchases of liquor, but also the usage. Any breakage, mistakes, or rejections from a guest are recorded on a waste sheet. You also have to account for bottles given to the kitchen manager for food preparations such as wine or brandy. Some places separate these items from FOH and BOH, but it can become too confusing when they are all locked up in the same liquor room and it is time to do inventory. You are not responsible to keep records on the food costs, which the kitchen does, but have to account for such things as food rejected by guests, dishes improperly or wrongly made, dropped on the floor, or guests changing their mind. Those things have to be recorded on a waste sheet or on the computer system as a comp. The kitchen manager needs that information in order to calculate his or her food costs and inventory.

Not knowing basic food costs, liquor costs, prep time, or waste costs will allow money to "fly out the window." Whole dinners are wasted, eaten by the staff, or given away to guests, resulting not only in more food costs but also increased labor costs because the food has to be prepared twice. People can literally take things home like liquor bottles, inventory items, and even raw meat cuts, etc. without you realizing it if nobody keeps track.

I once worked at a resort that did not do inventory. Not only did I witness bottles being taken, but also a full rack of ribs by the kitchen manager. One cannot imagine the waste, total costs, and problems associated with that.

Guest checks

I once worked at a place where we were not allowed to print or add anything to a split check. When a printer got jammed or ran out of paper, a manager had to reprint a check. I understand why we were not allowed to add anything because servers can be very creative when it comes to getting extra money, but they should be allowed to reprint the checks. It is unlikely that a check could be used for two different guests, and even if it was possible, you would have to reprint a check when a server asks, not knowing if they held onto it. This is where you must trust your staff.

When a server closes checks, any survey or other promotional information should be left off, if possible. It's just a waste of paper.

Evacuation plans

Every staff member should know what to do in a case of an emergency. This plan teaches the staff members to stay calm, going from one table to the next and quietly telling the guests what the situation is, ask them to leave the restaurant, showing them the way out, and where to wait outside. The calmer the employee appears to be, the faster it is to get people to go outside without harm.

The first table a staff member should try to approach is one that has children or elderly people seated at it. Printed layouts of the restaurant should be visible at certain locations to help employees to eliminate confusion or a stampede in case panic breaks out.

Once, the fire alarm went off while I was working, and nobody in the restaurant moved. People usually wait to take cues of what to do — stay or go — from the staff. We had no clue what had caused the alarm to go off, and only the fire department could turn it off. Because we had to wait for them to arrive and the noise was unbearably loud, we escorted everyone outside and did not let them back in again until the fire department was done checking out the building.

We all know that when people are completely done eating and they have the opportunity, they may leave without paying for their meal. You would want to train the staff to stay with the guests until everyone is escorted back inside again. Practice every once in awhile by asking questions like:

1. What would you say to a guest if …
2. Where would you tell them to go?
3. What exit should they use?

First-aid kits

This may sound like a "No duh," but one would be surprised to find that many restaurants do not have a proper first-aid kit even though OSHA makes periodic inspections. Most of the time items were never replaced after they were used.

Make sure that the kits contain everything that may be needed in a restaurant, including the most important items — burn medicine, finger condoms (no laughing, that is what they are called), and bandages. And not just any bandages; make sure they are water resistant. Every staff member will probably need one of this kind at some point. Always have backup boxes available, so the supplies never run out.

First In, First Out (FIFO)

Many managers apply this term only to food items because these items tend to spoil quickly, but it should also be applied to dry storage and other everyday items. Even though they don't spoil, they can become less useful through damage or becoming too dirty. (See "First In, First Out" in Chapter 6.)

Information boards

If the restaurant is using an 86 board, the computer system does not support this feature. Most computers will have this feature and will also have an item countdown feature. An item countdown happens when the establishment has only, let's say, five salmons left. Then, when a server orders one, the number of salmons left is reduced, eventually going to zero or "86."

Using a whiteboard or a cork board will let the servers know about drink specials, contests, and even who has a birthday, as well as items staff members want to share with others. This can make them feel like they are a part of a second family, not just employees.

Here is an example: When someone had a birthday and he or she was working, we put up a paper donkey on the cork board and played "Pin the Tail on the Donkey." Each part of the donkey represented a special gift: a day off, a special dessert, a meal, a section of his or her choice where he or she wanted to work, no side work, etc. Then the person was blindfolded and spun around. He or she would get the item on which he or she stuck the tail. We actually looked forward to working on our birthday. We knew that we could celebrate on another day.

Inventory

Just a note about "inventory" in general. Taking inventory is a must. It is a very tedious job. Here is an idea on how to go about it, which may help. To take inventory of liquor items you can post a sheet on the outside of the locked doors listing everything there is behind those doors. Then, when an item, or more, is removed, simply reduce the number on the bottle count on the sheet. When a shipment comes in and items are added to the contents, add the number of the new items to what was left. Double-check every two months or so. The same procedure can be used at other storage facilities as long as there is some measure of control.

There are four parts of inventory I like to mention, which are so important for FOH: glassware, dishes, silverware, and storage containers. Backups of all of these items should be stored somewhere, and here is why:

a) In most restaurants, the use of glassware means loss through breakage. Breakage happens not only when servers drop those items, but also when glasses come out of dishland too hot and are then filled with ice or cold beverages, because servers need them so desperately for the guests. Not even cooling them down under cool, running water helps. They tend to crack and break.

b) Again, dishes can break. Without dishes food cannot be served or eaten. Imagine not having a bowl to put soup in. In one place, we did not have enough bread plates. We would serve the bread on huge dinner plates. What kind of an impression does that leave on the guests?

c) Silverware tends to get thrown out. With too little silverware available the servers will run around trying to collect enough for the tables they service, or worse, they try to hide it to make sure they have some for their guests when they need it. In one place I worked we had to roll our own silverware for each table before a busy shift and again at the end of the shift. The shortage was so bad that these "rolls" were hidden in and around odd places in the restaurant including potted plants with stones on top of the dirt. The plants were used to separate sections.

d)   One can only imagine the reaction of the guests when a server is telling them that they don't have a container to put their take-out or leftovers in. Luckily, this happened to me only once, and the manager went to a restaurant close by and borrowed some. Some restaurants use better and stronger food containers for the take-out items and less expensive ones for the guests' leftovers. So, when they run out of the less expensive containers and have to use the more expensive containers, the company loses money. Having to run to a store to buy some can cost even more. It's always wise to have an extra supply on hand. This also goes for any other purchased item that does not spoil or has an expiration date. Make sure that the restaurant always has a sufficient supply in stock. But don't overdo it.

Logbooks

To use logbooks is one way to keep track of any event, which is happening in the restaurant that you might want to recall later or tell others about. A logbook can come in handy for multiple reasons, but there are a few very important ones a restaurant may want to keep:

a)   At the bar — A bartender writing everything down which happens in a bar can be very beneficial in any investigation, if ever needed. It can also be used as a communication tool to pass on information to the other bartenders. (More in Chapter 8: Bartenders.)

I once saw a gentleman walk halfway around the restaurant to the bar, order a beer, and drink half of it. Then he proceeded to go to the bathroom. When he returned he could barely walk;

he walked like he was very drunk. I called the police and then I wrote everything down, even a description of the man. The man had left before the police arrived. With the information I gave them they were able to track him down and take him into custody. We found out that the man had taken some kind of drugs, and they had arrested him before for that same situation.

b) A Manager Book or Computer Journal — This is vital for passing information from one shift to the next, or from one day to another. Checking the information before each shift and entering information before you leave should become a habit. Many managers do not do this. The problem is that people tend to forget to look at the computer or book when they first come in, or they forget to enter the information before they leave. This can cause staff to become angry with their managers because one manager does not know what the other manager did. In other words, the managers are not talking to each other, and nobody knows what is going on.

For example: One manager gives a verbal warning to a staff member. If the manager does not write this down for another manager to read, then the same person can get another verbal warning instead of the written warning he or she was supposed to get as outlined in the rules. On the other hand, if the manager wrote it down and it was read, the staff would realize that the managers are a team and are communicating with each other.

Believe it or not, this is very important for harmony in the workplace and to encourage the staff to respect all managers. Keep in mind that the staff will always test their managers to see if they communicate with each other or if they can get away with things.

You can solve problems as long as they use the logbook for what it is intended. Having the book also allows you to look back and reread the information you may have forgotten. Entering information into this logbook needs to become an important habit!

Another item entered in logbooks is forecasting. Forecasting is looking back to prior years to determine how busy the restaurant may be on any particular day. This information is put into the logbook temporarily and then transferred to a database or spreadsheet. All important information should be entered, for instance: date, lunch, dinner, weather, total sales, and local activities, etc. All of these have an impact on a forecast. For example: a snow storm would prevent people from going out to eat — unless they have snowmobiles or four-wheel drive vehicles (which actually happened in New Hampshire one year!) Other examples include: a theatre near the restaurant can increase business around show times, or a yearly festival can bring many new people to the area. Understanding how these examples will affect you business is essential to determine how many servers, bussers, cooks, etc. will be needed.

The next two logbooks are optional, but I highly suggest that they be used:

c) A book to track guests coming in to try to get a free meal.

d) A book that holds information on regular guests such as names, family members, food or drink preferences, etc. can help build clientele and help employees be more personable.

Log books can be used for anything the restaurant wants to keep records on, but they are only useful when other managers have access to them and utilize them.

Meetings

One out of many tasks you must perform is to schedule and attend meetings. A meeting is the most powerful tool available to you where you can talk about things that need changing, such as rules, regulations, procedures; what things work and do not work; general restaurant issues or problems; and upcoming events either in the restaurant or around town that may affect the flow of the restaurant, etc.

Manager Meetings:

These meetings should not just consist of the logistics of operating a restaurant such as statistics of last year's income, lunch/dinner, labor hours, costs, etc., but also of the personnel aspects such as staff not following the phone rules, what everyone is hearing about how staff is doing, or the need to keep an extra eye on someone. Discussing these things will ensure that all managers are on the same page and help create a hard-working, fun staff — and a generally happy environment.

Staff Meetings:

Every shift should start with a staff meeting. Staff meetings should not be scheduled to take place at peak times, and when a meeting is set, you have to make sure that other managers know the time, so they don't make everyone wait. Everyone should be punctual, and if a person is not, he or she should have to face consequences, because he or she will miss some important information. The meetings can last anywhere from two minutes to as long as needed. They should always be informative: about new menus, specials, new items, obsolete items, problems, and of course what the staff is doing right or what they need to improve. Make sure that the wrongs do not outweigh the rights since the staff is just beginning their day, and you want morale to stay high.

If you state a certain problem over and over again in multiple meetings, the staff members tend to tune it out, and it's a waste of breath. Make sure that everyone hears about the problem, but if it is not resolved after the first or second meeting, it's time for you to find out who keeps causing the problem and why it persists. For example: In one restaurant where I worked the servers would have to cut French bread for the guests they were serving. In order not to waste any bread, management told the servers to put the ends into the basket. Instead, the ends always stayed in the bread warmer. The floor manager did not catch the culprits doing it in the act, so he brought up the subject during the next meeting and the problem was solved. If this problem would not have been solved, the floor manager would have had to stay by the bread station to find out who did not follow orders.

In these staff meetings, all staff members should be tested periodically on their knowledge of the menu items. This could be done in a fun and interactive before-shift meeting or with questions asked of small groups during a shift in a "Did you know?" setting. If one person doesn't know the answer, ask another. If several people do not know the answer, they will be told that they will be asked again in the next shift they work. This way they will concentrate and will remember. For instance, they can be asked: "What is in our chef's salad?" "What are our steaks and their sizes?" "What sauce comes with the chicken?"— and so on.

Also, inform them about company specials like the distribution of coupons or about advertisements of special offers online or in newspapers. When a guest knows more than a server does, the company looks bad along with the server. Don't assume that your staff knows about them. Make sure!

Trainers must be informed about new food or beverage items that will be added to the menu so they can retrain the staff members in turn.

Minimum wages

Currently the federal minimum wage rate does not apply to tipped employees in most states. The hourly pay rates can be as low as $2.13, but differ from state to state. The biggest bulk of the employee's income has to come from tips in most states.

One thing which I would like to see happen in the industry is employers giving pay raises to their tipped employees as an incentive. This would accomplish two things:

1. Employees may stay longer at their place of employment, as long as they are treated well, which in turn would cut advertising and training costs for the company, not to mention that it can build teamwork and a sense of unity.

2. It would result in having better and more professional servers with more knowledge.

At this time people are hired receive the base hourly rate set by the state and/or the company, and they will leave their employment at any time when they are not happy with the job. But if they receive a raise now and then, they might just want to stay and try to help solve their issues.

Restaurants that are seasonal could give raises to employees who return every year. The same could apply to college students who return time and again to work during holidays and school breaks. Remember, you are saving on training costs, increasing loyalty, and creating more professional servers.

News and social media

Always keep up with the news to be informed about such things as how the economy is doing, what Congress wants to do about the minimum wage, how new laws affect the restaurant industry, or even what the new trends are. It is said that most of the food trends start in California, just like most of the new fashion looks come from Paris. You may want to keep up with articles and information published by the National Restaurant Association, LinkedIn, Wall Street Journal, and others that influence industry. You could even read periodicals on hospitality.

It is also very important to be part of social media. The restaurant should not just have a website but also a presence on Facebook, LinkedIn, and/ or Twitter. When it comes to search engines, try to make sure the establishment's website comes out on top and is easy to find. You can check Travelocity, Yelp, TripAdvisor, and Open Table.

I strongly suggest that someone keep watching these websites and comment on any bad or good remarks, and here is why: Bad ratings are unavoidable, but can be addressed by showing what has been done in trying to solve the problem, so everyone can read it. Through social media a person from the establishment can actually connect with the people who gave the bad rating and offer them a solution to the problem they experienced. If no one is checking the bad ratings or responding to them, those negative comments make the establishment look really bad and the situations will not be fixed, which will deter people from visiting your establishment. Make sure you also respond positively to good ratings to show that they are read and appreciated.

Encourage employees to use Facebook and to "like" the restaurant. Not only do they keep up to date with news about the restaurant and specials that are offered, but also it can bring new people into the restaurant and allows employees to tell their friends when they will be working — and maybe some of their friends will come in to see them.

Observation

Being a manager does not mean that you always have to do something physical. When you are not needed on the floor by guests or staff, take time out to observe. By observing you can learn a lot, like the flow of the restaurant, how the staff is handling the job, if someone is stressed and may need help, which servers are strong or weak, who gives outstanding service, and who has bad habits, etc.

Seeing and knowing all this will help with scheduling, knowing when to give help, or deciding when staff can be cut from the floor. When you are observing make yourself visible, so you can be approached when there is a problem and/or stop a problem before it can occur or escalate. You will also become more personable to the guests and become known to the regulars. (See "Touching tables" later on in this chapter.)

If you are coming to an establishment that already exists and has been operating under previous management, the one thing I suggest is to take some time to observe and figure out how it is operated, what works for them, and what doesn't work for them before trying to make any changes for the better. What works for one place may not work in another.

Open door policy

An open door policy means that every employee can discuss certain important matters concerning the company with their managers. Companies adopt an open door policy to receive feedback from their employees, so they can utilize the information to make changes in the workplace.

Have an open door policy not only to get employees' input on work-related problems, but also on any personal problems they may have.

If a staff member has a work-related problem, you could try to resolve it to the best of your ability. Never let employees walk away angry. They will tell others the reason for their anger.

If you can solve or just listen to your staff's personal problems, it could make them feel so much better, and, in turn, they will be able to do a better job even if the problem is not fixed. The FOH staff members are the face of the establishment and should always present a happy face to the guests.

Power outages

You have to make sure that your staff is well informed about what to do during those rare times when the power goes out. If the restaurant is fortunate enough to have a backup generator to keep the computers up and running, the staff will function better. But, if not, the staff must be able to do some of the following:

1. Check the status of every item already ordered
2. Know what alternative items can still be made, if any
3. How to write the tickets
4. How to turn tickets into the kitchen
5. How to look up item amounts and add tax, if applicable
6. How to process payments if credit cards are used and what information is needed
7. And most important, how to inform the guests of the situation

Being prepared will cut down on any confusion or stress when the lights go off.

Server break or must leave

If a server goes on a break or must leave for any reason and someone else has to take over, you should be informed and the new server should be introduced to the guests. Often, a new server will be assigned to a table, and the guests aren't even aware of it. They continue to look for their original server and can become very frustrated when they don't find him or her.

Server requests

When a guest asks to be served by a certain staff member it shows that he or she has done an outstanding job for them in the past. Serving them again is a privilege and should be considered a reward for a job well done. A server should receive a little extra when he or she gives a little extra.

Not all establishments allow this, but I strongly suggest this practice. Not only is the server grateful, but also the restaurant will benefit, because the guests will become regular guests and provide a steady source of income. These "regulars" are satisfied guests who tend to cause fewer problems. Can someone imagine a restaurant establishment which has all "regulars"? Let's see: steady income, happy servers, happy management, all due to fewer problems to deal with = The Ideal Scenario!

At one place I worked I had guests who would always request me. I was recommended other servers to them to ask for if I wasn't there. They knew that whoever I recommended would give them the same good service they were accustomed to. The guests realized that we worked together as a team and that everybody would give them outstanding service. They felt comfortable and did not mind asking for another server when I was not available. At one place the server happened to be my daughter. Can't get a closer relation than that.

Table numbers

Table numbers should start with a one. For instance — 11, 21, 31, and so on. Do not use a number like 10, 20, 30, etc. For servers to count quickly when they look at the tables in a row, they need to start with one. That way they can easily put the main number in front. For instance — in training they would say that the table is in row 10, 20, or 30. So, when a server has table 34, 44, 54, and 55, he or she knows that they are in different rows and the server can count the tables as 4, 4, 4, and 5 and put the corresponding whole numbers in front. This comes in handy. (See illustration below.)

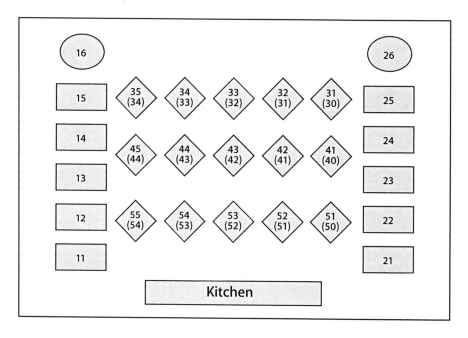

I once worked in a place that started with (10), (20), (30), etc. I always had to write down what table numbers I had to serve so I would not get confused. I happened to have table (31), (32), (41), and (51) and had to write down table 2 and 3, 2 and 2 for a visual look.

Teamwork

In order to promote teamwork you must have a group of people who are dedicated to making this work (See "Interactions" in Chapter 10). Usually these employees are trainers. They will be the eyes and ears when they are working on the floor. They will help to enforce the rules and motivate the others to work together. When the staff knows that the management team is behind the trainers, they will give the trainers their respect and follow their instructions. All trainers should always be introduced to new staff members, and they must understand that they need to listen to the trainers. Managers in turn must keep an eye on trainers to make sure they are following the establishment's rules and guidelines.

Touching tables

Always try to touch each table (literally) to get the guests' attention and to ask if everything is OK and to their satisfaction.

And while you are doing so, stop long enough to talk to them, to get to know them, and to find out their preferences, if possible. This practice will build clientele and create loyal guests. Their input might even help to get new suggestions for food and drink items. The guests would feel as important as they are to the company. Without guests there would be no business.

Chapter 10

Hiring and Keeping Employees

Finding new employees

For every new person who has to be trained, the company loses valuable money, which could be used elsewhere or to help retain them. Consistent staff members require no training, are reliable, cause fewer headaches, and overall make everyone else's job easier.

But if the establishment has to hire new employees, here are a few suggestions:

The best way to find someone would be to offer current staff members an incentive to bring in someone whom they know would be beneficial to the company. For instance: If a staff member suggests a friend, and if that friend is hired and stays for at least three consecutive months, the employee receives $50.

Hiring people that are older is a good idea because they have more experience, better understanding, patience, and are a bit more concerned with the running of the business. They tend to know what is important.

If staff members cannot find anyone, my advice is to ask them where they would look for a restaurant position. Past experiences have shown me that managers place ads where the staff doesn't even look. The most common place is Monster, but there are other places you can check. Some are listed in the appendix.

Resumes

Many young adults do not have a resume when they are looking for a position in a restaurant. That is why it is important to ask questions that would normally be answered on a resume. For instance, where did they work before, why did they leave, and if this is their first job, did they participate in any after school activities, were they a leader of a group, did they do volunteer work, etc. The information would be helpful in determining their character. (See the appendix.)

If the applicants have a resume, it will also give clues about their personalities and the knowledge they may have, which comes in handy in knowing which jobs are right for them.

Some establishments require online testing as part of the application process; the online application process may also enable an applicant to post his or her resume online. If the establishment has online testing for new applicants, you have to know what these questions are and how to interpret them. Not all questions may pertain to the present situation, so sometimes a person cannot answer them, or if answered truthfully, it may not be a real indicator of who he or she is. For instance: Many questions may pertain to his or her social life, but if someone just moved into the area, he or she may not have made any new friends yet. In that case, not having any friends does not mean that he or she is not a social or friendly person, which is what the questions may imply.

This actually happened to me. My job application was turned down. So I took my resume into the restaurant and asked for the manager. I told her where I came from, what I did before, and why I applied for the job. When she saw on my resume that I had 20 years of experience, we both had a good laugh over it. By the way, I was hired right away and started the following day. Meanwhile, she informed corporate about the problems of the online testing questions for new applicants.

Interviews

The number one question to ask applicants is: "What is your availability?" because if their availability does not meet the restaurant's needs, there may be no sense in continuing the interview. Unless you see a future potential in them because of their experience, you may want to try to squeeze them in some place. This also depends on how flexible your staff is. Their availability would be of vital importance to you when it comes to scheduling.

When looking for a host, most managers look for someone to answer the phones and seat people. How hard can that be, right? This is why people see many teenagers holding that position. If you think that no skills are needed, please read the host section in this book. It will show that a host is the most important functional person of the FOH staff. The host is not only the first person the guests encounter (and so gives guests their first impression of the quality of the service of the restaurant), but also he or she sets the pace for the entire restaurant. When hiring people for the position, you must understand the importance of the job and make sure that the person fits the role. Does he or she look the part? Is he or she smart enough to learn all the requirements listed in the host section? And so on.

When looking for a server it does not mean that you hire the first person who shows up for the interview just because you need someone immediately. A server should be picked carefully. Your staff is — or should be — like a second family. They rely on each other for support and the ability to do a good job. If one server leaves a bad impression on a guest, the other servers may not get the chance to make up for it and the restaurant loses a guest. Why would you want to take the risk by choosing a server who does not fit into the family? A staff that works well together will promote more teamwork and will always help you find the right person, if you let them.

To see if the prospective new employee is good at handling guests, you can ask what he or she would do in a certain situation. (See examples in the appendix.) You may want to watch for these things: Is he or she easy to talk to? Does she use proper English? Does he show good manners by using "Please" and "Thank You"? Does she make eye contact, sit up straight, and engage in conversation? Does he hesitate on questions, or do his answers come too quickly or seem rehearsed? Any of those three responses can mean that he or she did not think about what they were going to say.

You, or the other interviewer, could ask the candidates what their hobbies are to help understand what drives them. Certain questions can lead to valuable answers.

Many times, as a server, I would converse with the new potential hire while waiting for the manager to arrive. Through a short conversation with them I was able to place them into one of three categories:

1. **Yes** — Definitely friendly, good eye contact, excited to be there, curious

2. **Maybe** — Friendly, eye contact, but more reserved, distracted, or nervous

3. **No** — Unfriendly with an attitude "I am not here to talk to you"

As a manager, I once interviewed a gentleman who gave me all the right answers to all my questions. But after I left him to talk to my co-worker, I had the feeling that all he did was give me lip service. He gave me all the answers I wanted to hear, but they seemed to be too practiced and not flowing — just as if he was reading from a script. My co-worker noticed the same when he was interviewing him. When we checked the man's references and previous employments, we found out more unpleasant facts and were glad we did not hire him. Go with your gut feelings. They will never steer you wrong.

Many interviewers skip over the part to ask for references. But being able to contact and talk to a former employer or friend whose phone numbers the applicant may have supplied, and asking the right kind of questions, you can gain a clearer picture about the qualifications of the applicant. Make sure to get a signed authorization form from the applicant and, if possible, maybe an authorization to do a background check.

To get the best possible information about newly hired people and see if they are suited for the position, more than just one person should interview them. I suggest that you have a senior person, who is currently holding that position — or even two seniors separately — also interview them. I know, you might not think that this is such a good idea and say, "It's a manager's job and not a staff member's job," but think about the benefits.

The benefits could include:

1. The other interviewer might find faults with the applicant that you overlooked.

2. They may find that the new person does not fit into the work ethic or culture.

3. Their questions may find new results.

4. The applicant may become more open and relaxed answering questions because the staff member is not the boss.

5. If the staff members accept the new person, he or she will be readily accepted by all, hence creating the ultimate team-work environment.

If you are worried about the questions the other interviewers may ask, you can make a list with the senior members and have HR sit in.

Another deciding factor is the level of experience the applicant may have. If he or she has prior experience, you may want to ask the applicant what POS computer system he or she worked on. Of course, the more experience they have, the less training time that they will need.

After the interviews, all notes are presented in a meeting which allows open communications, and everyone can add his or her input to the interview results.

With the opinions of the other interviewers, combined with the impressions you have gained through the interview, you will be assured that you are about to pick the right person for the job.

Orientation

Does the applicant really want the job, or — better yet — can he or she do the job? This is where orientation comes in. Many people think that working in a restaurant is an easy job and easy money until they try it.

During orientation, the new employees have to understand what knowledge they must attain to be able to perform the job. Servers should be introduced to the menu, which includes sauces, substitutions, and allergies. In other words: Make them aware of all the information before training starts to help determine if the job is right for them. Introduce the host to the computer system and the complexities of all the duties involved.

The new employees must also understand what physical aspects they will need to perform. This can include lifting 40 pounds of heavy supply boxes and being on their feet for five hours or more without sitting down. They also should know what kind of conduct will be required, such as teamwork, rules and regulations, consequences if things are broken, etc. (See the appendix).

Inform them about the local area, and the history of buildings and their owners. Everyone should know if the restaurant is affiliated with other businesses in the area such as Outback and Fleming's, or Olive Garden and Red Lobster. The more they know, the better they can explain things to the guests.

After orientation, those who were given all the material and feel up to the challenge will remain and show up the next day. The hires who thought it would be an easy job may be weeded out. The more structured the orientation is, the easier it will be to attain good, hard workers.

Try to remember that the new employees are eager to learn and want to do a good job. But if the actions of other servers and managers are below standard, or if anything they are taught is not done on the floor, they will lose their enthusiasm. Give reasons for doing it the right way. Making sure that they will fit in with the rest and become a vital team player is essential. Remember that actions speak louder than words. Show them what your culture is all about, and don't just tell them.

Training

Before the training starts, you would want to make sure that an up-to-date training program is available and that specific staff members have been trained in it. (Training examples for hosts and servers will be given in the appendix, containing guidelines, useful information, and possible reasons why certain suggestions are made, for better understanding.)

Monthly meetings with trainers should be held, if necessary, to go over all the material and decide what should be changed, what can be improved, or what may be eliminated. Listening to the trainers gives the trainers a feeling of importance and pride, and they, in turn, will create the same feelings in the rest of the staff. You know that warm, fuzzy feeling. New employees can also give new insight to solving problems or making things easier.

When setting up a training program, make sure that you do additional testing at the end of each training day. This can include things such as computer information; information about the establishment's address, phone numbers, hours of operation, rules and procedures; food knowledge for servers,;and seating charts for hosts. After all that, you may be asking the new hire, "Are you still awake?"

Do not train or certify people, which is the last test, during peak hours, such as on Friday or Saturday nights. You would not believe how many places do this. The pace is usually too fast for the trainees to learn anything, and if the trainers slow down, the service to guests may start to suffer.

Remember, at the final test a trainer should only be available if absolutely needed. On a busy night, new employees can easily be overwhelmed. If you haven't noticed, this is why I am trying to stress the point of not doing any training or testing on busy nights. This might even be applied to "Hump Day Wednesdays" and "Thirsty Thursdays," if your establishment offers specials and the place is always busy. The term "sink or swim" is used a lot. But do you really want your new staff members to fail? Once the trainees complete their training and are certified, give them two tables to start with, even on a busy night. Test their skills slowly. Once you see that they are comfortable handling two tables, go to four tables or a complete section. This will also depend on their experience.

The same admonition applies to hosts — you have got to be kidding if you are thinking of putting someone who is brand new on the floor on a busy Friday or Saturday night. A host's job can be more stressful than a server's job. He or she will have to deal with phone calls, wait-lists, and guests who get angry because they have to wait. What the heck are those guests thinking? No waiting on a Friday or Saturday night! Really? But we all know that we get those kinds of guests. Again, you would want to ease him or her into their new position until he or she feels comfortable. Put the new hire as a main host on slow days and as a second host on busy nights. Once he or she knows what to do in critical situations, he or she should be able to handle anything that comes along.

It is also the perfect time to evaluate the trainer's performance after the trainer's class is completed and the new trainees are on their own.

Each establishment is unique, so the training program should be tailored to the needs of the company. Try to make training fun using visual aids and written information. This can be done with role playing, "What would you do?" games, taking guesses at what's in a particular dish, or telling funny stories about what really happened to someone while working. New people will look forward to more training and will be happy to come to work in the future.

A key to having a well-trained staff is testing the applicants to see if they are ready to do the job and to follow through with everything being taught.

When training, here are just a few details you may want to pay special attention to when distributing the training material to the trainers:

1. **Hot Schedules or other computer scheduling systems:**

   Once people are hired, the trainees should be trained on, and their names entered into, a computer program such as Hot Schedules, which will allow them to view schedules, pick up or drop shifts, and communicate with fellow employees and managers. Make sure they understand how to use this program! I have seen many times that, when a new server wrote a message intended for other servers, it went to everyone: hosts, bartenders, kitchen staff, and managers. Sometimes even a "private message" to a manager went to everyone. Not a good thing!

2. **Samples:**

Allow trainers to order small portions of a food item that is unique to the restaurant for a new server to try — unless there is a large group, then a whole meal can be ordered. This way they can not only see what it looks like, but they can taste it as well. This will help them describe and sell the items to the guests without having to waste an entire meal. I once was given the chance to try a veggie burger during a training class and loved it. I would never have ordered one before that because to me it did not look appealing.

3. **Pictures:**

Training should be as specific as can be. Showing servers what an item looks like and giving a description will help prevent alterations to an item like putting whipped cream on a dessert if it comes without it, or omitting the whipped cream if the item comes with it. Consistency is a must. If the establishment offers steaks, show them pictures of a steak showing steak temperatures with descriptions to help give accurate temperatures to the guests. Laminate all pictures to use over and over again, unless these pictures are given to each server in a training packet.

4. **Cheat Sheets:**

A great way to help the new servers when they are on the floor is to create what I call a cheat sheet. This is a small piece of paper listing menu items a server may not remember from training, such as all dressings, vegetables, side dishes, prices for substitutions, or sauces that go with certain items. These sheets can be placed in a server's notebook for easy reference, and they are usually done in an Excel format with grid lines. They can make servers look smarter and give them more confidence.

As a manager, and even as a server, I always put a cheat sheet in my training pack. When other servers would ask me, "Where did you get that?" I would tell them that I made it, and then print ones for them, too. Example below:

Salads Dressings	Lunch
Almond sal — Vin	Pasta — Alfredo, Sp. &MB, Lasag
Asian Sal — Sesame soy	Ravioli, Mac N' Chz
Cobb — Balsamic	Salads — Cobb, Santa Fe, Chinese
Dips	**Sides / Veggies**
Wontons — Sw. Chili	FF, Sw FF, Mash, BK, Rice
Tex Mex — Salsa	Broc, Carrots, Corn, Beans, Tomato
Ava Rolls — Tamarind	Spinach, Peas

5. **Menu knowledge:**

Start giving a server, bartender, or a take-out person menu knowledge, which is the most important and time-consuming aspect. They should not only state what is on the menu, but also how many ounces an item weighs (such as chicken, beef, or salmon), how many pieces of an item are in a serving (such as 10 wings or four cheese balls), and what could accompany a particular item. For instance: the sauces come with it and the ingredients in a sauce, what kind of cheese can be offered, what can be substituted, and if a substitution is made, if it is made for free or if there is an extra charge and how much the extra charge is. I have found that many places do not give this kind of information.

If you update the menu it is important for you to remember to let the staff know as soon as possible. I have worked in places where new menus were out and nobody mentioned a thing about it. I was stunned when I went up to my first table and the guests ordered a new item I did not know we had. Yeah, I can laugh now about it, but at the time it made me look like a fool, not to mention what they may have thought about the company. The servers are the ones who will be selling the new items. The more they know and learn about them the better off they and the establishment will be. To help sell the new items, give each server the opportunity to try them so they can describe them to the guests. Also, make sure that the servers know where the items are located in the computer system and if other items were eliminated.

Allergies

Servers have to know what is used in the preparation of food and drink items so they can advise their guests, if asked, on what items they can safely order, or offer to show them a separate menu, if available. For instance: If a guest is allergic to shellfish and he or she orders a hamburger, the guest may want to know if the French fries coming with the hamburger are fried in the same oil as the fried shrimp. Most restaurants use separate fryers, but it would be wise to check this out. Gluten, peanuts, nuts, dairy, and shellfish are just a few of the most common allergies.

I suggest, that you put a list together (like a cheat sheet) of the items on the menu that people cannot eat, divided up by allergy. Example below:

Dairy (not have)	Nuts (not have)
Beef Strog	Cashew Chicken
Pudding	Almond Salmon
Mac N' Chz	Brownie (walnuts)

I was bringing desserts out to another server's table one day (three adults and two children) when the oldest boy asked me if there were walnuts in the brownie. I said: "Yes." He answered, "Oh boy, my brother cannot have any because he is allergic to nuts." I told him to always tell the server when they order something, and explained to him how dangerous ordering food in a restaurant can be due to possible cross-contamination. I don't understand why people do not call attention to their allergies all the time. It just shows that they do not understand how the restaurant industry works — nor do they know how to tip. (I know! I just had to throw that one in.)

Alcohol

Knowing the beers and wines offered by the restaurant and a little bit about them will help servers to guide their guests to the correct choice when they are asked. They should also know the top three most popular alcohols in each category, such as vodka, gin, rum, and tequila.

This is important for young people to learn if they are allowed to serve at the age of 18 but do not drink. They may not have much knowledge about alcohol in general. We can pretend, right? That sip of champagne at a wedding or New Year's Eve does not count.

Cross-training

Cross-training is extremely important and should be a priority for those who want to do more. When the staff members know how to work in another related position in the restaurant, it is so much easier to do the scheduling or to fill in positions that are needed due to "call outs." For example: If a bartender calls in sick, someone can be taken off the floor to cover his or her position.

Being able to fill in for a host or for a take-out person when the need arises is a great example of teamwork. This practice, if chosen, should be stated upfront before a person even gets hired. Make sure that they can do the job they were hired for before any cross-training.

Make it clear to the staff once they are cross-trained that their main position is the original one they were hired for, and that, if they are called upon to fill another position in the upcoming schedule, they will be asked first. This will help eliminate problems when a server is asked to fill in as a host on a particular day. Then the server would know that he or she will get paid an hourly rate and will receive no tips. If he or she needs to work on the floor, he or she should be able to say so. Understanding, respect, and unity will play big roles here.

Also, if a host calls in sick and a server is asked to help, to show appreciation you can compensate the server somehow, maybe with a free meal or with the perk that he or she does not have to fill in again until everyone else has done so.

If you decide to cross-train someone, go through all of the training provided for each position so everything will be consistent. If you are fortunate enough to have the FOH and BOH staff working together, cross-training can also jump between the two groups. Cross-training builds understanding and teamwork.

Performance expectations

An important task is to review performance and expectations and present them to the staff. I know, staff members who have been in the industry may ask themselves, "What the heck is this?"

In my thirty years' experience, I think that it was done twice, OK, maybe only once, OK, maybe it was all in my head! But — in all seriousness — when you check periodically it will help you to keep restaurant standards up, help the staff to do a better job, and help you to get to know how well your staff is performing. You will have to get the information through observing, verbal questioning, computer data, and guest scores. Guest scores are highly overrated, though. The best is, in my view, when a guest goes out of his or her way to ask for a manager and tells him or her how great a certain server is. In most surveys the guests will receive a gift amount for their efforts and that is why they do it. But if people go out of their way and write on the credit card slip or tell a manager, they really show their appreciation. This is more valuable than a survey.

Performances are tasks you know but can improve on like increasing food sales, increasing liquor sales, increasing organizational skills, and getting better in how you present yourself to guests, interact with teammates, and handle any given situation.

Expectations are certain skills that need learned like knowledge about sanitation procedures, increasing menu knowledge, better guest service, or learning more about wine and beer. Other expectations may include coming up with new drinks (for bartenders) or completing a CPR class (for everyone).

Incentives

To motivate employees, you might want to look for some incentives to give them, for instance, increasing the hourly pay rate, paying for sick days after being there for more than one year, or paying for time off (PTO).

Another area is, for instance, when a staff member is "caught" providing exceptional service. This could be when guests write complimentary notes on their check or when they go up to the manager to tell him how pleased they were with their server. The servers could be rewarded with a free appetizer, dessert, meal, a day off per request, a holiday off, a gift card, or, if he or she has a long drive to work, with a gas card. Knowing and understanding the feelings of the staff can help you to come up with new ideas. These "out of the blue" gifts are such high morale boosters.

I once worked for a place that had us learn all about guest service, cleaning supplies, and safety. Each time we completed a program, got tested, and put it into practice on the floor, we received 5¢ per hour more. Another incentive was that the longer a person worked for the company, the higher was the hourly pay base. It may have only been a few pennies, but over time it will add up and create loyalty. We could also earn enough time off for any requested day with pay, or — the best one yet — even for a holiday of our choosing, with pay!

Some restaurants hold contests to increase sales or just to promote a certain item on the menu. Contests that work best are, for instance, who sells the most rib-eye steaks, desserts, or appetizers. The winner then receives that particular item as a prize. Another contest could be "Who can create a perfect check?" — meaning to sell an alcoholic beverage, an appetizer, an entree with an add-on like sautéed mushrooms or a special sauce, when it costs extra, plus a dessert or after-dinner drink, such as cappuccino, latte, or brandy.

Bingo, which some establishments play, is a bad idea, especially when played during prime time. Employees are constantly checking their bingo cards to see if they won because they have to be the first one to call "bingo." Then they are distracted from their jobs, efficiency suffers, and so does guest service. When holding any kind of contest, make sure the staff can do it without having a time constraint, time taken away from guests, or time taken away from doing the job itself.

Knowing what drives the staff at work or in their private lives gives you a great advantage. For instance: For some staff members, who may need all the cash they can make and already work two shifts, having a contest to increase sales where the prize is a free meal might be enough motivation. That way they do not have to buy a meal or bring food from home, and they save on their own food costs.

On the other hand, knowing what a staff member likes to do outside the workplace and would enjoy being rewarded with is also helpful. Some ideas include a dinner for two at the staff member's favorite restaurant so he or she has the chance to be waited on — or, if he or she is into sports, tickets to a local sports game.

Trainers should be given the incentive of being paid more per hour when they are training new staff members and possibly a free meal. This is to show appreciation to them for the effort and time they spend, and the knowledge they give to train others properly — the right way.

Trainers help create the atmosphere for the restaurant just like management does.

New staff members look up to trainers; trainers look up to managers.

Interactions

Make sure that you have a group of employees who function well together as a team in both the FOH and in BOH and will communicate any discord with each other and help each other, when needed. This is so, so, so important!

All staff members in their specific positions should be aware of what duties other people are doing and know how certain tasks interact with others in the restaurant. BOH kitchen personnel should understand the needs of the FOH staff, and the FOH staff should understand the needs of the BOH staff. That will, hopefully, create more respect and understanding between the two work groups. FOH staff will gain a sense of how fast BOH personnel has to work to get the orders out, and will be more understanding when orders come out wrong and have to be recooked. BOH staff will understand why FOH needs items and asks for things to "fly." This can affect the flow of the restaurant. The expo is very important here. (See "Expo" in Chapter 6.)

"On the fly" means an item needs to be made as quickly as possible, usually when it was forgotten or the dish was rejected by the customer.

In a place that did not have an expo I once asked a cook for a salad that was to be put in a special bowl, called a wing bowl. The cook asked me for the bowl, and I told her that we did not have any and that dishland did not either. She raised her shoulders as if saying: "Oh well, I can't get you one." I pointed to those bowls located behind her and asked if they would do. She ignored me. This interaction should not be allowed as a cultural norm.

When a cook asks a server for something (such as a plate, bread, or even something to drink), that server should get it, no questions asked.

I overheard a manager asking a cook to remake a salad and the cook said: "Why?" I was floored. Then I was blown away when I heard the manager explain everything to the cook. To ask the question is fine when the cook asks a server, but not a manager. This example shows that the cook had no respect for the manager, and the manager lacked authority.

Employee turnover

As already mentioned, the number one problem in restaurants is employee turnover. This whole book is written to help prevent it. Turnover is not cost-efficient — but the good news is that it's not difficult to understand why it happens. If you want to understand the business, you must understand the feelings of the staff. The more you know what drives the staff, the better you will be able to retain them.

One of the main reasons employees leave is because they feel that they do not get any respect. This is a big issue because most staff members are younger than 25. I believe that these young adults think managers look down on them — or that the managers do not know anything and therefore the staff members do not need to respect them. When management does not understand that **every** role in the industry is critical to the operation, turnover will always be high. If a dishwasher walks off the job, how will the restaurant get clean plates for the cooks to put the food on? And what will happen when the cook walks out, or the server, or the bartender? Keeping every staff member happy is probably an impossible task, but trying to do it is a must. Your staff may not know much about respect, but this is where you can teach them. If management fails to do so, they will not get any respect, either.

Here is an example: If a staff member comes in late for work, call that to his or her attention by saying, "You are late. Do you know that this shows a lack of respect to me?" This simple statement and question teaches them how to respect. At other times, say something like "I can respect that," or "Thank you for your respect." You are the ultimate teacher. My advice is, be a teacher so they will always remember you, just like I will never forget my 5th grade teacher, Mrs. Glass, who taught me a trick about how to remember the 9's multiplication table.

If the staff gets along with their co-workers, and everyone has respect for the other person's position, so must you show respect for the staff. As they say: "Respect is earned, not given," and when the employee performs well, he or she should get that respect. I know it is not easy when you need to enforce the rules and at the same time try to avoid becoming a bully. Listen to what the employee has to say about a situation, no matter how you feel about it personally.

You need to weigh your thoughts and opinions and let staff help you solve problems. This will make the staff feel part of the operation and not just single entities.

Another turnover point is when servers feel they are not making enough money for their efforts. This can be due to a number of reasons: business is slow, too many staff members are assigned to the floor, or — even worse — hosts are playing favoritism.

It is understandable that staff members don't make enough money when the business is slow, but if too many people are on the floor, it is a scheduling issue. (See Chapter 16.) The hosts who prefer certain servers and want them to make more money cause a tough problem. A host may seat the staff member he or she likes with guests whom he or she believes will produce more income or larger parties — or are known to leave generous tips.

This happens all the time, and if it is allowed to continue, the rest of the staff will feel cheated, they will become angry and hostile, and the morale will plummet. Not all people receiving this favoritism realize it, but it is something to watch out for. (See Part 2.)

The situation can be resolved by simply observing and listening to the servers, making sure that the hosts understand how to seat guests and that the head count of guests is fairly evenly distributed among all servers on the floor. To understand how to seat guests will benefit not only the staff but also the guests, because they will get proper service.

The best way to keep the people from leaving is for you to make sure they are treated fairly, are earning enough money, and to show them that you are trying to solve their issues and problems. This can be done by being approachable, listening to them, using suggestion boxes, and, of course, by making them feel that they are an important part in the restaurant's decision-making process, because they are. Even if you cannot solve their problems, your efforts to do so will be appreciated!

High management turnover

Having a high manager turnover is a sign to a server that there are too many problems. The staff will come into work saying, "What flavor of the month are we today?" When servers come into work and do what they were trained for and then have a new manager change everything, they will become angry. It will create discord among the staff. This is not a healthy situation for an establishment.

Some corporate restaurants have managers that are there for a year, and then they are moved to another store. This is to help prevent staff members from becoming too familiar with a manager, becoming a manager's favorite, or from being treated differently than their co-workers. This is different from changing managers every two to three months as described above.

Having a high turnover makes a staff member wonder why, if they keep seeing new managers. Remember, a restaurant's tone is set by the managers and then trickles down. The causes for them leaving might be:

1. They don't make enough money
2. The hours are too long
3. There is unfairness between managers (such some manager having to work more days than others)
4. A combination of all the above.

Owners must find a solution for this problem, just like managers have to find solutions to solve their staff's problems.

Exit reviews

As with performance expectations, you may be asking, "What the heck is that?" Keep in mind that when people leave they do not keep their grievances and reasons to themselves. You don't want to be the only person on staff not to know why a staff member left — especially if you can help prevent someone else leaving for that reason.

Exit reviews are often overlooked because people believe that it is the trend in restaurants that staff is always leaving to change jobs due to their whims. But exit reviews, if done properly, can be a wonderful tool and a good learning opportunity for managers.

The reason may be simply that they are moving away, going back to school, or to pursue another job opportunity in a different field. In these cases, it is important to keep the door open so they are allowed to come back in the future, and it also maintains a good relationship.

Maintaining a good relationship means that this person may give positive reports to others he or she encounters in the future. He or she may refer others to the establishment either to work there or to be a guest. And if an employee ever wants to come back to work for the company, the company would save the money it would have to spend for training a new person.

Other reasons for leaving employment may be:

1. Dissatisfaction with tasks they are ordered to perform, such as they have to do too much side work compared to the amount of money they are making, they are being forced to clean bathrooms when that task is not part of their job and they are not getting paid for it, or the company has them do things they do not believe in, such as consolidating condiments or reusing bread. Yuck! And yes, this does happen. Scary!

2. Unable to do the job properly because they cannot stand or walk for many hours, are unable to lift trays, or tend to make too many mistakes over and over again.

3. Being treated poorly by managers who are pointing out their actions to other employees as what not to do, or by other staff members not accepting them. I have seen this happening.

4. Not making enough money because they do not get enough tables or because other servers are treated with favoritism.

Each individual reason will be unique and so will be each solution. All those reasons, however, explain the turnover rates. To improve these rates one would have to get to the bottom of their complaints by asking them why they are leaving.

Knowing the reasons for a large turnover can help determine where your attention should be focused. The only way this will work is if you are approachable and convince them that nothing will go into their records and that you want to make things better. Sometimes, if you can solve their issues, they may just stay and give it another chance. **People tend to open up when they truly believe that you care.**

My advice is: Make life easier for yourself and everyone else. A consistent staff requires fewer training classes and easier scheduling, and gives you better reliability and better problem-solving. You can rely on employees to call on each other when they have problems either at work or at home. The results are: no more high turnover, a happy staff, happy guests, and fewer headaches. Good luck, and may the hospitality god smile down upon you!

I cannot stress enough the importance of knowing that the servers and all other staff members are the lifeline of the establishment.

Knowing and understanding what drives them is just as important as knowing and understanding what the guests want. Everyone knows that one bad report from a guest will spill over to ten other people, and that good reports do not stretch that far. This is the same with employees leaving their jobs. Whether they leave satisfied or dissatisfied, they will be telling family and friends about it.

Chapter 11

Good Leadership

*B*eing a leader is to lead by example. This is true in any position or any field. If you are in charge of someone and can't do what that person is doing, then you'd better learn how to do it or make sure that there are multiple people available who can. When the staff members see that you are willing to help them when they need help, and that you know what needs to be done, you will gain their immediate respect and loyalty, which is worth a ton of gold in this industry.

With this respect, you will gain loyalty, trust, and hard workers. Staff that looks forward to coming to work and are happy will radiate their happiness to the guests, who in turn will come back again and again.

I worked in a family-owned restaurant for many years and was told by my guests over and over again that not only did the food taste good but also that they loved that the staff was always smiling and joking around — not just among themselves but also with the guests. It made them feel at home and part of the staff, and they always had fun to boot. And let's face it, who doesn't like to laugh and have fun when going out for dinner?

Appreciation

Never take employees for granted! When you ask the staff to help out with something like folding napkins, take note of who actually does the task. If some staff members do something, anything that is not part of their job, or that is above and beyond, you have to make sure that they are acknowledged for it. Giving them a sense of appreciation will help to retain them as loyal employees.

Everyone knows that the servers are always caught in the middle of any bad situation, and here's why: They are the ones who have to deal with the verbal abuse from the guests. For instance, a guest may say "It's taking too long," "The food is overcooked (or undercooked)," or "There is something in the food." Then the servers get blamed, and the guests may give them bad tips or no tips at all.

The servers can also be verbally abused by the cooks when they accidentally order a wrong item or when they tell them not to add a certain ingredient. And even when they do things right and the cooks make something wrong, servers can get yelled at, or put down with a disgusted gesture.

Back up the servers whenever possible, so they do not feel like they are on their own. They would feel better coming forward with their problems. In turn, the restaurant would become more of a unit and more efficient, and not manager vs. servers or servers vs. kitchen.

But a host can also have multiple problems, such as dealing with angry guests who don't understand why they cannot be seated at an empty table they are looking at, even if it is dirty. People become angry when they have to wait, or when they call to be put on the wait-list when the establishment does not have call-ahead seating, etc. Let's face it, our society is becoming more angry, demanding, and impatient, and yet we have to be hospitable at more times.

The restaurant has only a minimal number of hosts employed. When a host calls saying he or she cannot come to work, you have to call another host in to fill the position. When that person does come in, you really need to show your appreciation because the employee is coming to work on his or her day off. The same should be applied to servers and bartenders.

Knowledge

The first time that I was holding a manager position in a family restaurant, the owner decided to cut back on the number of managers he employed in his three locations. He let a manager go from each restaurant. I was fairly new to the job but did not have to leave. The manager who was let go had been with the company for more than 20 years, but received a much higher salary than I did. I asked the owner if it was possible for him to keep her on, paying her the amount of my salary, and for me to go back to being a server. He agreed. She kept her job at my salary rate because she desperately needed it, and she is still with the same company today, six years later. After a while I took a manager position in a resort restaurant. Later, they also downsized, let all their managers go, and hired one person at a much lower salary.

After that I took another position as manager in a community golf resort. I tried to fix many of the problems they had, but after 10 months the general manager of the resort told me not to cut off people who had had too much to drink. I put in my two-week notice and told him, "Your restaurant is not worth five years of my life in jail if something should happen." To this day I don't think that he understood.

I tell you this because unfortunately many managers feel threatened by staff members when they try to pass on the knowledge they gained in previous positions. Many managers decide to go back to serving for different reasons. For instance: having flexible hours, being able to take vacations whenever they want to, possibly earning more money per hour, having fewer responsibilities, or even to pursue other interests, like writing a book.

The point is: Do not be afraid of the knowledge your staff members can bring to your establishment. Listen to them when they try to help solve problems and ask questions. A good leader knows that he or she can always learn from everyone, no matter what station he or she is in. Many individuals who have been working in this field for many years truly enjoy doing the job, and they also genuinely care for others.

Negative talking

It is also a good move to stop any negative behavior by stepping in and talking to the people involved. For instance: When the staff is talking about how they are not making enough money because there are too many people on the floor, that managers are never around when they are needed, or, even worse, that managers say one thing and do another, thereby implying that they don't care, this kind of talk will bring down morale. And the situation will only grow into more discontent, spreading to other staff members.

There will always be individuals who grumble about one thing or another, but if you genuinely try to solve issues, staff will see that and know that you are always listening, and in turn you will always have the staff's support. Intervene and address those negative behaviors at the end of the shift. If a person complains constantly it will bring down the mood and morale among the others and affect the guests.

When I was a manager and the staff was not making enough money in January (downtime) for the hours they were working, I asked the staff if they had a solution. What we decided was to put fewer people on the floor but at the same time cut back on the number of days each person worked, so, while on the floor, everybody would earn money. Another solution was that, with a consistent staff, they would take their vacations during these downtimes. Everybody understood that they needed to save money during the busy times in order to get them through these downtimes.

Productive staff

Have the staff trained to look around and do anything that might need attention before the rush starts. They will have a smoother running shift when everything is ready ahead of time. When you see that people are not doing anything, tell them what needs to be done, but in a respectful way. For instance: "Hey, Joe, will you please brew some coffee before we open?" or "Sue, could you please help Dan with the setup to get the restaurant ready for lunch?" If you like to hear "Please" and "Thank you," then you should also use those words. Promote teamwork every chance you get.

Seniority

Seniority is fine up to a point. People who have been there longer should get priority, but not at the expense of losing other, newer staff members because they feel that they are being pushed aside. New employees need to earn money, too. Finding a good balance between treating employees who have been there for a long time with the respect that they want due to their experience and encouraging new employees to fulfill their potential of becoming like the more senior employees is essential.

Strong servers

When people are talking about strong servers they may just be referring to servers who have food runners and bussers doing some of the work for them. All they really have to do is get the drinks, take the orders, put them in, and be attentive to the guests they are serving. That does not make them necessarily "strong servers." Some may be; others may not be.

The ideal "strong server" knows how to multitask. For instance, he or she knows the menu well, how to run food, and how to restock items; has mastered the computer system; and doesn't have a weak, slow pace. This can be done by forcing a new server to do all kinds of extra tasks, testing his or her knowledge, giving him or her the opportunity to serve large parties, and, in short, making more demands on him or her. One just has to be careful to give everyone the same opportunities. To turn the weak or new server into a strong server is to team him or her up with servers who can show them how to multitask. The goal is to turn every staff member into a strong server.

Chapter 12

Bad Leadership

Anger and frustration

Unfortunately, not every manager brings out the strongest service from his or her staff. Some managers often become frustrated and angry, not necessarily at the servers, but the staff can still feel their frustration. Some managers tend to blame the server, or worse yet, the server does not get any help from him or her in handling a problem. Try to understand that the servers get it from all sides and appreciate what they do. Appreciation and respect would go a long way.

I once put in an order for a salad. That salad disappeared from the window so they had to make another one for my order. Unfortunately, the salad I had ordered in the first place was supposed to be without dressing, which was told to the cook, but I guess he was not listening. The second salad they made had a dressing on it and was returned. The guest did not blame me, but did not leave a tip. The manager was angry with me and so was the kitchen staff because they had to make three salads.

Really? And how does that make someone feel? My advice is: The manager should have taken control of the salad and made sure that not only was it made properly, but also was delivered to the correct table and that the guest was satisfied. Without any necessity for him to get angry, all problems would have been eliminated.

Hovering over

Hovering over the staff members to make sure that they are doing their job properly or taking over their jobs is a bad move. Not only can you make them nervous, but also you can make them feel worthless.

Once, a manager at a restaurant where I was working went up to a table and asked the guests if they would like another glass of wine. Meanwhile, I came up from behind and asked the same question. They told me that the manager had already asked. The manager got distracted and never ordered the wine. How did that make us both look? This undermines the server.

It was not the manager's job to ask the guests what their wishes are. Managers can ask if everything is OK and let the server know if they need something, without the manager taking it on. That way the server will know what he or she needs to do.

I have seen a lot of times when a manager has walked behind a host's desk and started talking to the guests, telling the hosts where to seat them. This is not the manager's job. If the hosts are overwhelmed and do not know what to do, try to help and guide them so they learn and become better at their job — don't take it over. Remember, the most important job a manager must do is delegate and follow through.

Humiliation

It is in very bad taste when a manager, who holds a superior position over another manager, humiliates him or her in front of a subordinate. A server should not have to listen to one manager putting down another manager because of his or her inflated sense of self-worth. Not to mention that a manager makes the server angry or upset, and then the server has to serve guests who may sense that anger. He or she will also lose respect for such a person and will not want to work for that manager. A situation like that would defeat any term of "hospitality." Can you tell that this happened to me?

It happened when I was working as a server. The regional manager came in, joined the general manager of the restaurant, and ordered five different items from the menu. They were discussing one particular item when the general manager went to check the ingredient on the computer. When she came back she told the regional manager that he was right. The regional manager then stopped me as I was passing by and asked my general manager to repeat to me what she had just said. The general manager was very humiliated when she repeated: "You were right." The regional manager smiled at me and put his hand up in the air like he wanted a high-five. I looked at my general manager and proceeded on my way not acknowledging the hand. Because I had been a manager before, I was so angry. I wanted to wipe his smile right off his face and give him a piece of my mind, but I held my tongue — another thing that I've learned how to do.

Hypocrisy

Telling a person how expensive something like straws are and then ordering the staff to put new straws in every refilled drink instead of asking the guest to keep his original straw is being a hypocrite. You will lose respect instantly. Be careful.

Unfairness

If you are not fair the employees will not give you the respect you deserve. For instance: I was working in a restaurant one day when only two servers were on double shifts and eight others on single shifts. I was scheduled for a single shift. We were not busy all day. So, I went up to the manager and asked if I could stay on a little longer than the other people scheduled for a single shift. This is the response I received: "Well, everyone else has to make money, too!" I felt that this reply was a complete lack of respect to me and a put down of someone who just wanted to work. My question here is, "Would this have made you a little angry?" Would it not have been a better reply to say 'I can try?'" Think about the way you talk to people. In my case, I lost respect and the will to do my best for the company.

Here is another example of unfair treatment. While the inspectors from OSHA were watching, an employee was cleaning the hand-washing-station with a towel from a sanitizer bucket — evidently because the sink needed wiping. The restaurant received negative points for this. The manager yelled at the employee for cleaning the sink, thereby practically blaming her for receiving a negative report from OSHA. I'm not sure what the OSHA employee was thinking, but I do know that even hand-washing sinks need to be wiped down from all the soap being dispensed. The assumption, I believe, of both the manager and OSHA employee was that the towel that was being used was not sanitized. The manager could have talked to the person to find out if the towel was sanitized, and if it was, to tell the OSHA employee. How else can one clean a sink that has just been used by servers to wash their hands? Even if the employee was not within OSHA standards, whatever they may be, the manager should never yell. He or she should explain to the person what he or she did wrong so it does not happen again.

It is important to respect the employees and treat them fairly, because they may be unhappy with the treatment, or, even worse, the establishment may lose them. Without employees, the restaurant cannot survive, and you would be out of a job.

Unhappy employees will also project their feelings to the guests and others around them. Now, I am not saying that you can please every employee, but that you should try.

Many managers believe that, because they are the manager, they do not have to explain themselves. Yes, this is true, but in some cases it is important that the staff understands your actions. For instance: When you assign a large party to a server who is not in rotation because the guests had requested that particular server, you would want to explain this to the other staff members, so they will understand the reason and not become angry.

Chapter 13

Problem Solving

*W*e've heard it all before: how much the staff is appreciated, how much the managers care about the staff, and of course, how managers will fix all the problems that the staff bring up. Right? Well, saying all that is fine, but usually it goes into one ear and out the other, because most managers do not listen properly and do not try hard enough to understand every situation. Listening and acting are the key in obtaining a staff that trusts one another and works hard and well together.

Deal with it

Problems can arise anytime, anywhere. Any job that involves the human element will have them. We are all human with human shortcomings. It's how we deal with solving the problems that makes or breaks the atmosphere. Problems in a restaurant, work-related or personal, do affect everyone there. They will have an impact on guests, staff, and loyalty (perhaps leading to high turnover), just to name a few possibilities.

Whenever a problem arises, it is important for you to learn what the problem is and come up with a possible solution. Listening to the employees and trying to help them will earn you a solid, hardworking staff. Yelling or getting angry shows lack of control. Talking down to or punishing a staff member for a simple mistake will tear down every-thing hospitality stands for. It also doesn't solve anything. I mention this because I have seen it happen too many times.

It does not matter how a problem started or who was involved in the problem. If you are talking to the person with a problem, then you own it. Any staff member dealing with a guest's problem must try to solve it by himself or herself, or find someone who can help him or her. Make sure that your staff understands this.

Staff members are not the only ones who get angry or frustrated. As a manager, I have dealt with many guests that were downright rude, mean, and — no matter what I tried — were not going to be satisfied. These things do happen, but the one thing I remember is that not only did the other managers understand, but also that the entire staff was behind me. As a manager it's nice to hear a server say, "Yeah, she's got your back, and we have hers," instead of hearing, "She is too soft — there are no consequences for broken rules, she is too friendly with the staff, or she is not a role model because she does not know how to do our jobs." Being able to show authority but at the same time have a caring hand and a listening ear is a skill that all managers should master. Just because you care, it does not make you weak. If anything, caring makes you stronger.

I once had a server who could not stay off her phone. We talked, and I told her to go home and get whatever she needed under control in her life, and that once she did she could come back and talk to me. I took her off the schedule for about three weeks. When she came back I put her on the schedule again. One day when I was in another room, she walked by talking on her phone again. I shook my head; she kept walking and never came back. She was caught and learned the consequences.

We all get upset over things that do not go well, but keeping calm and addressing the problem in a meeting either before a shift, after a shift, or both, if possible, will be more beneficial. These meetings can provide a lot of useful information for everyone. One thing to remember, though, is not to turn it into a bashing segment. Allow staff to express their ideas, opinions, and concerns without retaliation. This also creates respect between staff and management.

I have worked at places that held two meetings: before a shift started, about specials and new menu items, and then again after the shift, in which any problems that were detected were discussed, and the manager took the opportunity to tell the staff what a great job they did to sell the new items and specials. Meetings like that made the employees aware of the possible problems that could arise and know how to prevent them from re-occurring. Because problems can be handled in different ways having the staff bring ideas into the discussion can help find better solutions or reveal other potential problems. (See "Meetings" in Chapter 9.)

When trying to fix a problem, make sure you do not create another one! If the staff is not doing something they are supposed to do and you decide to try to fix it, make sure you do not hurt the other people who are doing the tasks. For instance, if you decide to give fewer tables to staff members who are not acknowledging the guests quickly enough or who do not keep up with their side work, make sure that you are not doing the same to the rest of the staff.

Arrangement with guests

Never comp something without going to the table first. If you were called to a table to talk to guests and made any kind of arrangements to appease them, such as comping the meal or offering dessert, make sure that you inform the server of that fact. Even if you did not have to take any action, because the guests were the best guests in the world, still let the server know what happened so he or she will feel more relaxed and a part of the process.

Short for "complimentary," meaning "free," a "comp" could be any item that needs to be taken off the bill for any reason.

Problem guests

If a server has a problem with a table and he or she cannot go back to it because of a specific reason, try to evaluate the situation and either assign another server or finish serving the table yourself. Try to support the server in the decision he or she had made.

Dealing with problem guests can be very trying. Know the servers well enough to know what they would or would not do. If guests become verbally abusive, remove the server from that situation and tend to those guests yourself. Do not assign another server to such a table.

I had two incidences when I was working as a manager:

1. A server came to me crying and explained what happened. I told her not to worry about it, to go to the bathroom and freshen up, take some deep breaths, then go and take care of her other guests. I served the problem guests from the beginning to the end and gave the server her tips. She was new at the job, but was very happy and appreciative, and she became one of my best servers.

2. I came up behind a server when I overheard the guest say to her: "You are stupid and cannot even do your job right." That was all it took. I moved the server to the side and said to the guest: "I am sorry that you feel that way, but you don't have to verbally abuse (name) that way." I told my server to attend to her other tables, then continued telling the guests who I was, asked them what the issue was about, and told them that I would be taking care of them through the rest of their meal. After I finished, they apologized to the server and me, saying that they had a bad day and took it out on the server.

A suggestion on how to cultivate clientele that does not promote problems is to be personable with them. Try to get to know the guests by asking questions like: "What is your favorite meal (or drink or place to sit)?" Learn if they have any family living in the area. These questions help to establish a connection, and because of this connection the guests tend to complain less and visit the restaurant more frequently (See "Logbooks" in Chapter 9.)

Free stuff

Sometimes giving free stuff away or replacing food for disgruntled guests when the staff does something wrong is unavoidable, but there are people who want something for nothing and come up with all kinds of ways to get it. They realize that they can get a free meal if they complain, and they take advantage of the restaurant's policy to always try to please a guest each time they go out to eat. Sometimes it is so blatantly obvious what they are doing that it borders on the ridiculous.

I had one guest who ordered a baked potato topped with butter, sour cream, bacon, cheese, and chives. The person opened the potato, smashed it all up, and laid a hair on the top stating that she found it in the potato and that the hair came from the server. It was a dark hair — while the server's hair was a natural light blond — and it was not inside the potato but laid on top.

Here are three things that you could do if the establishment does not want to deal with that kind of clientele — that is, if you feel comfortable doing so:

a) You could say: "I'm sorry, I see that you have mashed up the baked potato, and the hair is not coming from the inside of the potato." You can pull the offending hair off and say: "I will get you another one." After replacing the potato with another one you can say: "There you go," and walk away.

b) Make a mental note of what the guests look like and watch for them the next time they come in.

c) Try to get their name from their credit card and enter the incident with any notations into a logbook, showing the dates the guests were in, what they ate, what free meal or replacement they received, or if anything was done at all, etc.

If they repeat their ploy, you can make a second notation, and when they do it a third time you can try to stop it by approaching them, stating all information collected from previous visits, and telling them simply: "I'm sorry, but it seems that every time you come in here we can't do anything right. You may be better off being served in a different restaurant from now on."

I have seen managers from one restaurant get together with managers from other restaurants in the area and share that type of information. It can work.

Chapter 14

Rules

*A*ny owner or general manager has to set standards and give written guidelines that everybody in charge can understand and uphold. In these standards and guidelines, include everything you want the employees to know. For example, explain what happens when a rule is broken, when a uniform does not meet the code, or if they do not show up at a meeting, etc.

The employees should know what the consequences are when a rule is broken, for instance:

> 1st offense — Verbal Warning
> 2nd offense — Written Warning
> 3rd offense — Suspension
> 4th offense — Termination of Employment

It is important that you enforce all rules, procedures, and policies — and those items should be discussed with all staff members, or better yet, written down and handed out. Written copies of rules, regulations, and guidelines should be handed to each employee during or after his or her training.

Certain rules that are already practiced in the restaurant are mentioned in the establishment's handbook. Make sure that the staff goes over those in a training session.

Of course, all rules and regulations should be realistic, not stupid. Have reasoning behind them and make them a standard for all employees, not just a selective few.

All managers should be "on the same page," so all will enforce the same rules. If one manager tells the staff not do something, and then they see that another manager is allowing it, they get confused, or — even worse — they don't care about rules because they are always different. It is human nature that if someone sees somebody else do something and get away with it, to try to do the same. "Monkey see, monkey do."

All rules, regulations and guidelines mean nothing if they are not enforced! (This will break down respect and unity.)

Broken glass bins

Place bins in dishland for servers to use, and put another bin behind the bar for all empty bottles. This will help to avoid any possible injuries.

When I was working one day as a bartender, I grabbed a tall, black trash bag and flung it up into one of the garbage bins out back when it hit the side of the bin. The bag bounced back, and a broken glass bottle cut through the bag and hit my forearm. Needless to say, the cut was so deep that I still have the scar.

Consistency

Written standards, graphs, and guidelines can help show how things should be set up and lessen confusion. Everyone will do things the same way. And when guests order something, it won't look different from the previous time when they ordered the same item. All staff members should be consistent when it comes to such things as coffee setup, hot tea setup, number of pieces of bread in a basket, folded napkins, when and how to use trays, and especially standards on food — for instance, how to serve desserts, whether with whipped cream or without, with ice cream or not, and, if it does come with ice cream, how many scoops. This is very important when servers have to do it themselves. Some establishments allow servers to omit or add items to a dish, and others will not. Make sure that the establishment's practices are clear to all staff members. This includes restaurant setup and teardown.

Cutting gloves

Enforce the rule that everyone uses a cutting glove. These are special gloves that help prevent accidentally cutting oneself. This should not pertain only to cooks, but also to bartenders and servers who have to cut lemons, limes, bread, etc. It will save the employees from unnecessary injuries, and save a lot in workers' compensation costs.

Favoritism

Favoritism is probably the biggest problem in many restaurants. It leads to anger among staff, low morale, and the loss of great servers, which results in having a high employee turnover. This subject should be stressed in training sessions. If someone gets caught doing it, they should face consequences.

As mentioned earlier, favoritism comes into play when hosts seat more tables and bigger parties with servers they prefer, thereby allowing them to earn more money. Other servers see that this is happening and become angry. They start talking negatively to other servers to get their support, and morale starts to go down. This eventually leads to good servers leaving their employment to find jobs elsewhere.

A manager can also practice favoritism by scheduling favored employees for work, setting up sections for them, or even by listening to people they like and following their ideas and not the ideas of others.

At one place where I worked as a server, I gave a manager my idea and never got a reaction. I then told one of his "favorite servers" the same idea to present it to the manager. The manager acted on it immediately. I immediately lost respect for the manager.

When it comes right down to it, if servers are not making enough money, they will move on. If they are making enough, they may overlook favoritism, but the negative talk will continue, and they will look for a better place to work. The restaurant will have no unity. Servers will always move on until they find the place where they can earn money, have a good environment, and receive respect.

There are three ways to prevent the problem:

1. By producing reports which show servers' sales and number of people served. If over time you see a pattern of higher numbers of guests and in sales for certain individuals, that may give you a clue.

2. By using the counting system explained in the host section
3. By observing

Marrying condiments

If the employees in the establishment are practicing this, make it a rule not to do it. Not only is marrying condiments against the health codes, but anytime something is combined it also becomes a big health risk. For instance: putting old ketchup with older ketchup. That means that the old food just keeps sitting there getting older and more dangerous. It will never leave the container. Yuck! No wonder people ask for new bottles or containers! In one place, we had regular guests who insisted on getting a new A-1 sauce bottle with an unbroken seal every time they came in. Now I understand why!

Parking

A rule that most establishments have and that new employees need to be made aware of is that they have to park far away from the building in a designated place. This rule is difficult to enforce because:

a) it is hard to catch people when they are parking closer to the door, and

b) the older staff members also try to bend the rule by parking closer to the restaurant. This sets a bad example for new employees. Tell them that they will be sent home when they are caught the first time and may be terminated when caught the second time. That might just get them to park where they should.

Phone usage

Phone usage is becoming a massive problem. Everyone nowadays has a phone, and many establishments do not care and allow their staff to carry their phones around.

Employees should not have a phone on them when they are working. Allowing phone usage can be a distraction and lead to a lack of guest service, attention, and productivity — not to mention that it looks bad in front of guests.

In a meeting, you can explain to the staff how bad it looks when they are on the phone and how distracting it can be. And if you do not want to come across as a dictator or mean person, you could soften your explanations with a joke everyone can relate to. If the establishment has lockers for jackets and personal belongings (which would be ideal), tell them to leave their phones in there, or, if not, they can leave it in the car. If they carry their phones on them and want to use them during their breaks or between shifts when they are not working, they can go to the back of the restaurant where guests cannot see or hear them. Make sure, though, that making or answering their phone calls during working hours does not become a habit.

Chapter 15

Guidelines

hese are standards that can determine a course of action that can be changed based on the establishment's needs.

For instance, when a server who has finished serving the guests and is no longer required on the floor, the guideline can be for him or her to start doing side work. Another guideline is that a host will say, "Good afternoon, thank you for calling ... (name of the restaurant), my name is ..., how may I assist you?"

Here are a few suggestions that may be important to have as guidelines:

Assignment of sections and seating

When you assign servers to sections, make sure they are also aware of any closed sections around; not only do servers have to know which tables to attend, but the host also needs to know. I have seen many times that the host will seat people in closed sections. Everyone needs to know what is going on to be able to give the best possible service.

Another guideline you might want to make is not to seat a new party over six people until everybody is present. This is because larger parties tend to occupy a table for an extended period of time if the entire party is not present. Then the table cannot be flipped, and the server cannot earn any money.

Bus pans

If the establishment uses bus pans, you will want to make it easier for the dishwashers by setting them up in a way that promotes faster unloading. For instance: using one pan that only holds glasses and silverware, another one for small plates, and the last one for large plates. You will also want to make sure that the servers empty the plates of any food or sauce before putting them into bus pans. If dishes are brought back to the dish room, the guideline for servers and bus-people would be to stack same size plates on each other etc. The better organized the dirty dishes are, the faster the dishwasher can clean everything. The easier you can make it for the staff, the more likely they will stay in your employment.

Food costs

I have seen many times that guests will order certain food items from the menu and ask for all the ingredients to be served on the side. For instance: The guests may order nachos, which can be served with salsa, jalapeno, green onions, guacamole, and sour cream, but they are only interested in the nachos with cheese, or they order a baked potato and only want it served with butter instead with sour cream, bacon, cheese, and chives. They do not touch the other ingredients. To avoid those extra food costs, the servers should ask the guests if they really want all the other items on the side. Guests don't realize that they can order those items without the extra ingredients. In the long run, you will keep your food costs down.

Kitchen

Even though the kitchen is not your domain, it affects the FOH. Therefore, get together with the kitchen manager and set guidelines for the kitchen setup, which is often overlooked. For example, if the establishment makes food items like salad dressings and sauces fresh every day, the kitchen staff should know the par for the upcoming shift and have everything prepared and ready to go. This can eliminate running around, and making items in a hurry, prevents the kitchen from going down, and helps servers to meet any FOH setup requirements.

"Par" is the established amount of an item needed for a particular day.

Mistakes

Staff members will make mistakes. It's human nature. Having a set of guidelines can help people understand their mistakes and can help them not to make the same mistake twice.

Of course, everything depends on the severity of the mistake. A case where someone enters the wrong table number into the computer is not as severe as a case where someone enters the amount of a payment to the wrong table. In the first case, you would try to find out why it happened and quiz them on table numbers until they get it right. In the second case, harsher actions may be required. If minor mistakes continue to occur, you may want to sit down with the person to find a possible reason and to see if there is a way to help him or her.

When a server does something wrong and causes a problem, it is your job to make the entire staff aware of the problem, because if one person is doing it, others may follow. For instance: If someone automatically puts a lemon in water and the others see or hear about it, they may start doing the same, and the costs for the lemons would have to go up.

You just want to make sure that you don't single out the person who made the mistake or draw special attention to him or her. That would make the staff member very uncomfortable.

Sanitation

There should be some strict rules to follow for sanitation purposes. Cleaning supplies must always be kept away from food or drink items, and the sanitation buckets used for wiping down tables should never be placed next to the drinking water pitchers. Yes, I do see this a lot! Also the water in the sanitation buckets should be changed every two to four hours depending on usage.

Chapter 16

Scheduling

 cheduling employees for an entire work week can be a manager's nightmare. Here are some suggestions:

Consistent schedules

I found that one way to relieve the stress is to set up consistent schedules
for people who work the same days and same shifts week after week.
Being on a set schedule allows them to not only know when they will be
working, but also when they can make doctor appointments or schedule any other activities for the days they are off. Many times, I found
that, if they wanted to go on vacation, they would find people to cover
their shifts several months ahead of time, knowing that the favor will be
returned sometime in the future.

Also, if you schedule, for instance, 20 people for a busy Friday or Saturday night, try not to schedule that many people for other, slower days. With fewer people, even if people call in sick, you want to feel comfortable knowing who can handle more tables and who cannot. I see this happen over and over again. Staff is standing around with nothing to do. Remember, idle time means more mistakes are being made. (See "Overstaffed" later on in this chapter.)

Floaters

You might want to have people in your employ who are floaters. Floaters are people who have a wide range of availability. There are two types of floaters:

1. The person who has only two set days off per week. For instance, on Tuesdays and on Saturdays. They can work every shift on all other days, or

2. The person who wants two days off per week, but does not care which ones.

Schedule versus availability

"Being Scheduled" and "Being Available" mean two different things. It is funny how these two things always get confused by managers. Some people may want to be scheduled for every Friday night but not for a Saturday night, but they may be available and willing to come in on a Saturday when needed. My suggestion: Do not exploit this, or they may not be willing to help anymore. The key is to always ask.

Conflicts

Conflicts arise when you need people to work certain shifts, but no one wants to be available. Holidays are one of those conflicts.

Most places close on Christmas and Thanksgiving Day, unless the restaurant is connected to a hotel or resort. When the restaurant is closed for those two holidays, people are still needed for Christmas Eve, New Year's Eve, and New Year's Day.

One way I have handled this situation is by having sign-up sheets. How many a.m. and p.m. slots will depend on the number of staff and the number of shifts that need to be covered for the size of your business.

The diagram below is for a restaurant that will be closed on Thanksgiving and Christmas Day.

	X-mas Eve	NY Eve	NY Day
Server	a.m.	a.m.	a.m.
	p.m.	p.m.	p.m.
Bartenders	a.m.	a.m.	a.m.
	p.m.	p.m.	p.m.
Other			

The diagram below is for a restaurant in a hotel or resort, a place which is open year-round. If the establishment uses food runners and/or bussers, slots for those entries would also be needed.

	Thanksgiving	X-mas Eve	X-mas Day	NY Eve	NY Day
Server	a.m.	a.m.	a.m.	a.m.	a.m.
	a.m.	a.m.	a.m.	a.m.	a.m.
	p.m.	p.m.	p.m.	p.m.	p.m.
	p.m.	p.m.	p.m.	p.m.	p.m.
Bartenders	a.m.	a.m.	a.m.	a.m.	a.m.
	p.m.	p.m.	p.m.	p.m.	p.m.
Host	a.m.	a.m.	a.m.	a.m.	a.m.
	p.m.	p.m.	p.m.	p.m.	p.m.
Other					

You would be surprised how well these sign-up sheets work.

At one time, I worked over the holidays at a resort as the restaurant manager and did the sign-up sheets. I put one up, and by the time I needed to do the scheduling, the only shift I could not fill was the bar shift on Xmas morning. When I approached my bartenders, they all looked down. I told them what the problem was and that I would do it myself. The expression on their faces was priceless. After that incident, whenever I needed a server or bartender at the last minute, they would be there for me. Talk about gaining respect and loyalty (and unity). I had been there for only four months when this happened.

Another way is to tell staff to write down what shifts they would like off in order of preference. In this case, nobody would know what days people requested to have off. This would allow you to schedule people at your discretion without causing antagonism.

A third option you might try is to put all of the servers' names into a "hat" and pull out their names one by one, starting with the a.m. shifts. The person whose name has been pulled has to work. This might also help to resolve any conflicts and to be unbiased. I never used this method, so I cannot say if it works.

Double shifts

When scheduling people for double shifts , make sure that there is a good half hour of downtime between the shifts. You may want to check the labor laws in your state, because this may be a requirement. To arrange downtime makes good common sense and will allow the person to wind down and to grab a bite to eat. This kind of scheduling will also help when one is trying to avoid overtime hours.

Working as a server, I once was scheduled to work from 11:30 a.m. to 5:00 p.m. for the lunch shift, and for my night shift I was scheduled to work from 4:00 p.m. to 8:00 p.m. This was not only impossible, but I had no break and no lunch!

Also, when scheduling workers for double shifts, you would want to make sure that the tables are assigned to them fairly. Staff members will get very unhappy if they were assigned to a section that only has booths and cannot seat more than four guests at a table in the lunch shift, and then are passed over at dinner time on big parties because of the host playing favorites. If they did not make enough money in the first shift, they should be given the opportunity to make up for it during the second shift by being assigned to a section that is preferred by guests and that can accommodate large parties. If this happens, in the future they will be willing to work all day.

Many servers only want to work nights because the restaurant is busier, more food is being served, more alcoholic beverages can be served, and thereby the totals on the guests' checks, on which tips are calculated, are higher.

Servers will also become angry when they come in early and spend time to set everything up for the next shift before they can start serving tables and the host seats other servers coming in after them in busy sections and with large parties.

When scheduling breaks for employees working double shifts, look to see at what stage servers are with their tables. Are all of their guests almost done eating, or did they just get seated? The servers who are almost done should go first, and then you can slow down seating for the others.

Events

Before making a schedule for the week, make sure that you check everything that is happening in your community and around the area like sporting events, either in the area or on TV; festivals, shows and plays; exhibitions and conventions, etc. Make sure to think about **any** event that may affect visitor turnout at the restaurant.

Standby shifts

Some establishments have people on standby, which can be a generally good idea because it helps when someone can't make it in for their shift.

People on standby have to call in to see if they are needed on the floor. These are things to think about when scheduling.

Here's an example of the complexities that standby shifts can pose: Kim was scheduled for the lunch shift, to come in early and open the restaurant, and for standby for the night shift. She lived about 45 minutes away from the restaurant, and the manager was aware of that fact. After lunch, Kim asked if she was needed that night and was told, "I can't make that decision; it's too early."

Kim now had three choices:

a) to go home and call in later, hoping that she was not needed that night (she would have never made it back to work in time),

b) ask a closing server if he or she could take the spot and thereby be able to stay until the manager would give her an answer to her question, or

c) to just wait until the night shift and fill in the time with shopping locally, socializing, or reading, etc.

Knowing the needs and circumstances of your staff can help you with the scheduling. (By the way, as it turned out, she picked (b), and the manager started scheduling her for closing shifts when she was put on standby.)

Sufficiently staffed

If it is known that a large party is coming in for lunch, or an event is going on in the area, you may need more kitchen staff, servers, and bussers. Too many times I have seen that more servers were scheduled, but only the three original cooks were scheduled. The food will not come out in a timely manner.

Overstaffed

Be careful not to overstaff, which creates inefficiency. Workers tend to run into each other or stand around doing nothing. When staff is not focused and multitasking because they are not busy, they tend to make more mistakes. This fact is known throughout the industry!

Knowing how many tables each person can handle can help you to staff accordingly. Keep in mind that servers are trained, and are expected to handle four tables at a time comfortably. For instance: If you have four servers available and each server can handle four tables, you can seat 16 tables. Would you think that guests would walk in all at the same time to occupy those 16 tables? Try to estimate how many guests might come in at any given time and how many servers may be needed. You only need four servers if all guests for all 16 tables walk in at the same time.

Short Staffed

This can occur due to callouts, mis-scheduling, or even accidents, etc. You then have to make sure that all tables are assigned even if they are not all seated. This will accomplish two things:

1. It makes a server responsible for all tables assigned to him or her, and thus he or she will keep an eye on the empty tables, and

2. If guests come in and seat themselves, which we all know can happen, then at least someone is watching the table and will attend to them or get help.

This is also a time when you should jump in and help, if needed.

Outside seating

Scheduling staff for outside seating is really difficult when the establishment is located in a region where the weather cannot be predicted accurately. It can change from sunny to rainy in a heartbeat, or it can happen that it is sunny in one place, and the next town over experiences pouring rain. Don't you just love how the weather can make your job harder?

My advice would be that, if at all possible, you leave a couple of tables open inside or have a section closed so that, if it starts raining, servers can move inside with any outside guests. This same closed section could also be used for outside servers when it is too cold, hot, or rainy, so that they will not have to be sent home without having had the chance to work. Their time is just as valuable as anyone else's.

Another suggestion would be to post a sign at the front door of the restaurant and at the host station, which informs the guests that the patio will be closed. Then the guests can decide if they want to take the chance on the weather. They also should know that, if there are no tables available inside, they may not find a seat if anything happens.

On any day, keep in mind that tables located in the sun with temperatures around 90 degrees will probably not get seated. Those stations could be adjusted to have fewer servers assigned to them. The same can be done when it is too cold and the tables have no heaters — or when it rains. All these factors can help you decide what to do.

Scheduling for the patio

Because schedules are done at least a week, if not more, ahead of time, you may want to have staff members call in when the weather is questionable, and then ask them if they want to come in just in case, keeping in mind the distance a person may have to travel to get there. Or, you could just simply cut down on outside staff and have inside staff jump in when needed. This is a difficult problem, but knowing what the staff can handle may help in the decision process.

So, to make the lives of your employees less complicated, you want to keep their situations in mind when setting their schedules. If you schedule a person for more than one shift in a day, you would want to take care that the ending of their first shift is as close as possible to the beginning of their next shift or standby shift. Scheduling for a single, opening, closing, or standby shift should present no problem if the rest of the day is wide open.

Whatever happens that is unforeseen, make sure you feel comfortable that you and your staff can handle it.

In this situation — and in all others — be part of the team and not just the boss. Listen and jump in to help when the need arises! Understanding, respect, and unity all start with you!

Whatever stage you are in — host, server, bartender, or manager — enjoy your job. Your guests will respond positively to your open, caring heart.

Appendix

References

Server Training Program

New servers should receive the following items during orientation:

Menu	Rules and procedures
Script (skit)	Side work lists
List of expectations	Cheat sheet
Dining room nap w/table numbers and sections	Meat temperature pictures

Trainee will be paid minimum wage. All tips will be given to the trainer for his or her efforts.

Skit Example: Hello, How (are you) (is everyone) doing today? My name is ___, and I will be taking care of you. Have you been here before? If yes — "Welcome back." If no — "Welcome to (restaurant name)," then proceed to tell them a little about the menu and give them other important information. Tell them about any specials being offered and if the restaurant is out of anything. **Always** say your name, a welcome of some sort, specials, and any 86'ed items.

Example of a Training Schedule for Servers

Day 1

➡ Instruct the trainee how to clock in and out using employee number — touch screen, swipe card, and/or both

➡ Hours of operation; affiliations, if any; address; and phone number

➡ Uniform standards

➡ Procedure on who to call and when, if need be, if sick, late or unable to work, or have suffered an injury

➡ History of restaurant or of owner; if applicable, local activities

➡ Walk through the restaurant to locate dry storage, food storage, beer/liquor, soda, glassware, tables, etc.

➡ Functions of each station: host, server, bar, to-go, and kitchen stations

➡ Spend time in each area and talk with someone in that area to learn how that area works and how it affects your job. This can be broken down over multiple days.

➤ Review menu: item details, options, special orders, and up-selling

➤ Order and critique items

➤ Test

➤ Clock out

Day 2

➤ Clock in

➤ Check uniform

➤ Have the trainee observe kitchen, dishland, and expo, and ask questions about how things are made

➤ 30 minutes in dishland, so the trainee understands the importance of scraping plates and organizing dishes

➤ Have the trainee expedite food, work with the kitchen and service staff to get what's needed for items, read all modifications, and how to transfer (bump) items from one computer screen to another

➤ Go over steps of service

➤ Have the trainee practice carrying trays: empty glasses and full glasses, then empty plates and full plates

➤ Train on the computer in "training mode" (if applicable) with training sheets

➤ Review menu; order and critique items

- Go over side work lists: End of shift and running side work. Pick one for each training day to complete
- Discussion of the day for 15–20 minutes with the trainee and the manager on duty (MOD)
- Test
- Clock out

Day 3

- Clock in
- First part of the day: the trainee will run food to tables with and without a trainer or equivalent
- Go over table numbers
- The trainee should be 100 percent positive that he or she is running the right food. If not sure, he or she should always **ask**
- **Second part of the day will be spent at the host station; go over the dining room map, sections, computer, wait-lists, counting system, etc.**
- Go over steps of service; be descriptive
- Go over payment methods: credit cards, gift cards, comps, and deletes
- Phone standards
- Go over the buddy system

- ➜ Game plan on where to start seating and rotations. **Remember, the host runs the dining room. Communication with the servers and kitchen is important!!**

- ➜ Side work lists

- ➜ Computer training

- ➜ Review menu, order and critique items

- ➜ 15–20 minute meeting with the trainee

- ➜ Test

- ➜ Clock out

Day 4

- ➜ Clock in

- ➜ Check uniform

- ➜ Discussion about steps of service

- ➜ Review placing orders on the computer

- ➜ Payment methods

- ➜ Side work list

- ➜ Discuss power outage: how to write guest checks, get payment information, item look-ups with tax (if applicable)

- ➜ Follow trainee and observe: greeting guests, seating, flagging tables, delivering drinks, taking orders, delivering food, up-selling, delivering checks, thanking the guests and closing out a check

➜ When the trainee has served before give him or her a maximum of two tables to serve

➜ Review menu; order and critique items

➜ Test

➜ Clock out

Day 5

(Skip day 5, 6, and 7 if the trainee has served before. Continue with Day 8.)

➜ Clock in

➜ Check uniform

➜ Discussion about steps of service

➜ Practice with trays

➜ Review computer training and processing payments

➜ Role Play. Chance to do steps of service in a controlled atmosphere

➜ Side work list

➜ Review menu, order and critique

➜ 15–20 minute discussion of the day with trainer and MOD

➜ Test

➤ Clock out

Day 6

➤ Clock in

➤ Check uniform

➤ Discussion about steps of service

➤ Practice with trays

➤ Computer

➤ If you feel that trainee is ready: Follow the trainee and observe him or her performing all aspects: greeting, seating, flagging tables, delivering drinks, taking orders, delivering food, up-selling, delivering the check, and thanking the guest and closing out the check; if not: repeat days four and five

➤ Two tables max; go over organizing and saving steps

➤ Go through side work list. **A clean restaurant makes for an exciting experience for both guests and staff!!**

➤ Review menu, order and critique items

➤ 15–20 minutes' discussion of the day with trainee and MOD

➤ Test

➤ Clock out

Day 7

➤ Clock in

- Check uniform
- Discussion about steps of service and payment
- Tray practice
- Follow the trainee at a distance and observe him or her using all steps of service. Maximum four tables
- Supervisor and other staff members will answer any questions and give assistance
- Side work: Make sure that every surface is touched and work with others to complete the entire list
- Review menu; order and critique
- 15–20 minutes' discussion of the day with trainer and MOD
- Test
- Clock out

Day 8

- Clock in
- Check uniform
- Discussion about steps of service
- Time behind the bar: going over all the beer, liquor, and wine the restaurant offers

→ Time with bartender and trainer, waiting on a guest, making beverages and mixing drinks. Trainee should take notes, which could be helpful later when up-selling to the guests.

→ **Reminder: Trainee will still be taking orders for bar guests, so he/she must use all steps of service put in place**

→ Serve MOD lunch/dinner

→ 15–20 minutes' discussion of the day with trainee and MOD

→ Brief test on menu, standards, and alcohol

→ Clock out

This completes the training. The trainee will meet with the General Manager to discuss any concerns and progress. These meetings will be held at the end of the third week and again after 30 and 60 days.

The trainer should remember that every person absorbs information differently. This program could be adjusted to meet the needs of the trainees to help them become great servers.

Some trainers do the scheduling for trainees, so they will know who they will be with and when. When scheduling new servers, they should try to put them next to people who are more experienced.

Training Sheet

When making training sheets, the manager or trainer should list about 50 examples of the restaurant's food items, using lots of modifiers for both food and drink items. He or she can make things look complicated and even give some examples where the trainees have to ask for more information. For instance: If there are two types of sliders on the menu, only "sliders" could be mentioned, or if the restaurant offers more than one club sandwich, only "club sandwich" can be listed. Once all 50 examples have been completed, the trainees can work on 10 more each day. These training sheets can be used over and over again for new trainees. They do need updating, though, from time to time when the menu is changed.

Examples:

> Seat 1 — Coke
> Seat 2 — LIT
> Seat 3 — Absolute Martini w/ BC olives
> App. — Calamari
>
> Seat 1 — Kid's Mac N Chz
> Seat 2 — Chicken Alfredo, extra sauce on the side
> Seat 3 — Filet, M-FF, No Asp., Sub Broc
>
> Seat 1 — Kid Sundae
> Seat 2 — Brownie, Sundae, and Cof
> Seat 3 — Carrot Cake and Latte
>
> Payment — Cash, CC, Gift Card, Traveler's Check

Examples of Test Questions

Following are some more general suggestions for trainers on how to test and what questions to ask when testing:

- Each day, take food items and ask either what is in the food or what comes with it.
- Each day, review what was taught the day before and build on that.

- Start training by teaching easy tasks, and then move on to more complicated tasks.
- In the staff meetings before the shifts, go over any menu items and question the trainees.
- Have the trainee give you one glass of white wine, one glass of red wine, three beers from tap, and three in a bottle.
- Ask questions about stations and specials.

Here are examples of other, more specific questions:

- What do you do before you get the first guest?
- What is the greet time and check-back time?
- What are the steps of service?
- What does "86" mean?
- What does "on the fly" mean?
- Why do we say "behind you"?
- What is our phone number?
- What are the hours of operation?
- How do we set up for tea?
- What are our dressings?
- When do you have to show up for your shift?
- What is the call-in rule if you cannot come in for any reason, or if you are sick? For example: two or four hours before shift starts.
- What does the uniform consist of?
- What tools do you need to carry?
- What do you do when a guest's steak is undercooked?
- What do you do if someone delivers the wrong food?
- What do you do if you accidentally spill beer?
- What do you do if the plates or silverware is dirty?
- What do you do if you cannot get to a table?

- What do you do if a guest's beverage glass is half full?
- What do you do when someone orders a steak?
- What do you do when you see that a group is taking pictures?
- What do you do when you hear the phone ring and nobody is answering it?
- What do you do when you see people waiting at the host stand and no host is available?
- What do you do when guests are walking out without their to-go boxes in hand?
- What do you do when the supply of to-go boxes is running low?

Server Checklist

Restock:

- ❑ To-Go Items
- ❑ Coffee/Decaf
- ❑ Tea and Tea Kettles
- ❑ Soup Spoons
- ❑ Soup Items
- ❑ Ice
- ❑ Straws
- ❑ Napkins
- ❑ Printer Paper
- ❑ Ketchup and Other Condiments
- ❑ Plates
- ❑ Bread
- ❑ Glassware
- ❑ Butter
- ❑ Silverware

Restock and Clean:

(once a day or once a week)

- ❑ Salt and Pepper Shakers
- ❑ Sugar Caddies

Clean:

- ❑ Highchairs/Booster Chairs
- ❑ Tables
- ❑ Chairs/Benches
- ❑ Fixtures
- ❑ Soda Machine (and put together)
- ❑ Computer Screen
- ❑ Sweep
- ❑ Trays

Things to Do:

- ❑ Brew Coffee and Tea
- ❑ Get Ice
- ❑ Polish Silverware
- ❑ Bread Station — Bread, Knife, Patty Paper, Duck
- ❑ Cut Lemons and Limes
- ❑ Fold Napkins
- ❑ Sanitation Buckets
- ❑ Salad Station: (if required) Dressing, Condiments, Plates
- ❑ Soup Station: (if required) Soup, Soup Toppings, Bowls, Spoons, Small Plates,
- ❑ Liners, Ladle

List of Teamwork

➜ Assisting Orders-To-Go staff members

➜ Filling water or soda glasses, not just on the tables a server is assigned to, but also on the other tables around them or tables they are passing

➜ When seeing another server with hands full of dirty dishes, taking them out of their hands

➜ While cleaning one table, noticing other tables around them and cleaning those, too

➜ Restocking whatever is needed and not waiting until things are all gone

➜ Taking an order for another busy server and putting it into the Point-of-Sale (POS) System or getting the order to the server

➜ Giving change to other servers when they need it

➜ Greeting and getting the drink orders for guests of a server who is not able to at the moment

➜ Running food or drinks

➜ Asking if someone needs help

➜ Helping dishwashers

➜ Getting plates for cooks

➜ Getting drinks for cooks

➜ Getting food items from the pantry for cooks

→ Cleaning tables around your section or other tables that you are passing

→ Cleaning a mess, especially when it is not your mess

Host Training Program

The length of time needed for training will depend on the practices of the establishment and the knowledge of the trainee. I would suggest a minimum of five days for a person to learn the ins and outs of everything involved.

Day 1

→ Table numbers and floor plans

→ Answering the phone

→ Table orientation

→ Restaurant layout (where everything is)

→ Some computer training

Day 2

→ All of the above

→ Seating using the counting system

Day 3

→ All of the above

➜ Gather information to give to the main host, like open menu count, stages of tables, (clean, dirty, to-go), etc.

Day 4

➜ All of the above

➜ Beeper system

➜ Call ahead/reservations/heads' up

➜ Wait-list

➜ Bathroom checks

Day 5

➜ Manage host stand under trainer's guidance

A note on computer training: The trainer should make sure that the actual training starts slowly by showing the trainee only one or two things at the time. Then, on each training day, the trainer should review what was learned in prior days. This will ensure that the trainees understand what was previously taught before moving on and more things are added. If, for some reason, the trainee does not quite understand, repeat that day's information again testing him/her at the end.

Host Checklist

Checklist for the main host:

1. Get the server station layout from the manager or supervisor on duty. If no manager is available and you are allowed to assign

stations yourself, make sure that all reserved tables are set and that all servers know their assigned stations

2. Find out about any additions to the menu and 86'ed items, and inform the guests when they ask

3. Get wait-list, people count, and bathroom checklist

4. Maintain reservations

5. Always greet the guests in a professional manner

6. Try to stay in rotation using "people count" as best you can

7. Try not to leave the door unattended for any period of time. Ask another host or manager to cover for you if you must leave

8. Say "Good-Bye" and "Thank You for Coming" to all guests when they are leaving

9. Determine pace of seating

10. Keep track of wait times

11. Beeper system

12. Mark tables "available" or "unavailable"

13. Answer the phone

14. Get information from kitchen, hosts, meetings, and servers

15. Maintain supplies

16. Instruct other hosts of what is needed

17. Check table orientation

Checklist for all other hosts:

1. Stay in constant communication with the manager throughout the shift about wait times, parties that need to be sat, or any other situation that may come up

2. Check all menus and make sure that they are up to date and clean

3. Put tables together

4. Lead the guests to their table and make idle chat

5. Pace steps to guests

6. Remove any extra place settings

7. Bring a high chair or sling, crayons, and kids' menus, if needed

8. After two minutes of seating the guests make sure that a server has been to the table

9. Check stages of tables

10. Open menu count

11. Roll silverware, if that is part of the job requirements

12. Bathroom checks

13. Empty trash bins in bathrooms and host stand

Checklist for two hosts on duty:

1. Report to a manager or supervisor

At the end of the shift, clean menus and host station, organize everything, replenish items depleted, and inform the manager.

List of Interview Questions

- On what days can you work?
- Do you have any physical problems that we need to be aware of?
- Have you done this type of work before?
- Did you use any computer programs like a POS system?
- Why did you leave your last position?
- What did you like most about your last job?
- What have you learned from previous positions?
- What do you know about our company?
- What does good service mean to you?
- Why do you want to work here?
- Why should I hire you?
- What are your strengths?
- What are your weaknesses?
- Give me an example of a problem and how you solved it.
- How much money are you looking to make?
- Where do you see yourself in five years?
- What are your hobbies?
- What is your favorite food?
- Do you have any siblings who might want to work here?
- Do you have any questions?

List of Rules

- Broken Glass Bins
- Consistency

- Cutting Gloves
- Favoritism
- Marrying Condiments
- Parking
- Phone Usage
- Tardiness

List of Guidelines

- Assignments of Sections and Seating
- Bus Pans
- Checking Food when it leaves the kitchen
- Checking Shift-Leaders
- Update Side work
- Kitchen
- Problems/Mistakes for servers
- Position Points
- Scraping Plates
- Teamwork
- Uniforms

List of Manager's Exit Review Questions

- What is your primary reason for leaving?
- What part of your job was most satisfying?
- What part of your job was least satisfying?
- What did you like most about the company?
- What did you least like about the company?
- Do you feel that you were treated fairly and with respect by managers? If not, please explain.

- Do you feel that you were treated fairly and with respect by the other staff members? If not, please explain.
- Were you always able to get satisfactory answers to your questions and help with any problems?
- Did you like the working atmosphere and attitude of your co-workers?
- Were you engaged in teamwork?
- Did you find the rules and regulations easy to follow?
- Were you ever bored doing your job?
- If you were a member of the corporate team, or a manager, what would you like to change?
- What did you like, or dislike about the training program, and did you always get the support you needed?
- Were you able to earn enough money to meet your needs?
- Would you recommend this restaurant as a good place to eat?
- Would you recommend this restaurant as a good place to work?
- Would you ever consider coming back? If not, please explain.

Job Boards

www.monster.com
www.hcareers.com
www.indeed.com/Postajob
www.Linkedin.com
www.snagajob.com
www.careerbuilder.com
www.localjobsindex.com

Online Support

HotSchedules - This site is for managers. They help with finding new employees, programs for training, software for scheduling, logging daily information, getting industry news, and even blogging.

Career Builder and Local Job Index - These sites are for staff members and managers. They allow you to post your resume and help find the right job.

National Restaurant Association - This is for managers and staff. This website has the most extensive amount of information on everything pertaining the the hospitality industry.

LinkedIn - This is for managers and staff. The largest professional networking site full of industry leaders with all kinds of information in articles and a place to ask questions with those in you industry.

Restaurant Terminology

86: The restaurant is out of certain items.

Auction Off: When a server holds up a food item, names it, and looks for the person who ordered it. No, it does not go to the highest bidder!

B & B: Bread and Butter, not Bed and Breakfast places.

Bank: Small bills and coins to make change for guests. Not enough to steal, so don't bother.

Behind: Say "Behind" when walking behind another person so he or she knows someone is there. No, it is not that kind.

BOH: Back of the House: kitchen and dish room. Sorry, no garden and swing sets back here.

Born on date: The date on which items are made. Stop putting the sticker on you, you are way too old and will be tossed out!

Bullets: Small plastic containers that hold small items such as ketchup, cheese, jalapenos, etc. Careful not to give to the bar; they try to put them with the gun. (See below.)

Bump: When cooked items appear on the screen to signal that they are ready to be served, they can be selected and bumped or run to the tables. Keep hip movement to a minimum.

Buried: When a server is extremely busy and has too many things to do. Hopefully, not six feet under already.

Busing: Is when all items are removed from a table after the guests have left. Stop looking for the big yellow thing.

Butt Rags: Napkins used to pick up hot plates, clean up messes, and wipe fingers with. Please no wiping butts.

Butterfly: A thick steak cut in half lengthwise with a small section still together. It doesn't fly away unless it's thrown.

Call Ahead: When people call before they come to the restaurant. So much better than calling too late.

Campers: guests who sit for a long time and the servers cannot make money. Don't you just want to flip them?

Comp: "Short for complimentary (free)." When an item is made, has to be thrown away, and taken off the bill. The word is not short for "computer."

Corner: Something yelled when coming around a corner and you can't see. Or maybe someplace bad tippers go?

Covers: Menus. Not something to warm a guest.

Cut Off — Guest: When a guest is overindulging. He or she will find that the source of alcohol is missing and their keys are gone.

Cut Off the Floor: When a server does not have to serve tables anymore and is allowed to go home. YES.

Dishland: A place in the BOH where dishes are cleaned. Not an island I want to go to!

Drop and Run: When a host shows new guests to a table and leaves right away. Pushing and running not allowed.

Drop Check: When guests are done and ready to pay the bill, the server leaves it on the table. Please don't literally drop it.

Duck: A rubber device that fingers go into on one side and the thumb on the other to protect fingers while cutting bread. It looks like a duck's beak — really. Not to be used in bathtubs, only in dishland!

Esos: Extra sauce on the side. One can be a little more saucy when one wants.

Expo: Short for expeditor. A person who helps to put the food dishes together to be run to the tables. No, the expo does not have a booth and is not selling anything.

False Wait: When a manager tells the host to let guests wait before seating them until the kitchen is caught up, even if empty tables are available. Beats having a false start!

Fire: When the server is ready for the kitchen to cook the meal. Please don't yell that out loud.

Flipping Tables: A server takes care of one table multiple times serving different guests. The table is not flipped over to see if there is gum under it.

FOH: "Front of House." Public area where hosts, bartenders, servers, bussers, etc. serve the public. No gates and picket fences in front.

Full Hands In or Out: Servers should always have their hands full. If you have nothing to carry, look around and find something — just not a guest.

Garnish: Fruit or vegetable bits and pieces, little umbrellas, etc. Umbrellas, really? They are cute but would not cover an eyeball, let alone a head.

Gun: A device that dispenses nonalcoholic products to make drinks. It is always found behind the bar, so be nice to the bartender.

Heads' Up: When guests call ahead to let the restaurant know that they are coming in with a large group. You will have to recognize them by their necks.

High Top: A table that is raised above other tables, usually in the bar area. Watch for people wearing turtlenecks.

House Shift: A section on the floor that a manager could not fill and is offering to anyone who wants to come in and work. Shake it, don't break it.

In the Weeds: The same as buried or going under. Maybe in the weeds instead of water?

MOD: Manager on Duty. If the MOD reads this book, you will find one. Otherwise: Happy Hunting.

Monkey: A small dish used for sauces, butter, or other small items. They do not swing from trees; but they may hold banana slices.

Newbies: New employees. Not kids that cry or scream; OK, maybe some do.

On the Fly: A forgotten or rejected dish that needs to be made quickly. The food is not served on a fly and no throwing it. FOOD FIGHT!

Open Menus: The number of menus the guests are still looking at before they order

POS (Point of Sale): A computer that is used when selling items. Quit pointing at me; I am not for sale.

Pre-busing: Is when unwanted or no longer needed items are removed from a table when the guests are still present. Load them up early.

Regulars: guests who come in often enough to be known by their names and some personal information. They would be "irregulars" if they had digestive problems.

Rocks: Ice cubes. No rocks to climb and slip off.

Runner: A person who brings the food to the guests. We tried to slow them down to a "walker," but no one was going for that.

Running Side Work: Doing side work which has to be done throughout the shift. If it's getting away from you, better catch it.

Rush: When a lot of people come in within a very short period of time, usually during lunch and dinner hours. It does not mean "Hurry, I am hungry," or "Sorry, I didn't mean to rush you."

Scoop: Pick up food with a utensil or napkin without touching it. Don't try it on guests. They tend to get angry.

Service Bar: A place where the servers pick up the drinks for their guests. No, the drinks are not for them.

Shift Leader: A person who checks out the other servers to make sure that they have done all their side work. If you ask me, some of the people are a little shifty.

Slammed: When a restaurant goes from having no guests to having a full house in a matter of minutes. For a server, the term refers to buried, going under, or being in the weeds, just ten times worse

SOS: Sauce on the side. Not an international call for help.

Standby: A server scheduled for a shift he or she may not have to work. Isn't that typical of a manager?

Stiffs: People who do not leave a tip. Not a corpse (even if one would wish they were one), and get your mind out of the gutter.

Table: The term refers to either an object or guests that have to be served. Run that food to the table and see if it eats.

Training Wheels: A shot of tequila with salt and lime. When you are old enough we'll talk about removing them.

Two, Four, or Six Top: The number of people that can sit at one table. No matter what the size of the people

Up: Drinks served without ice in the glass, so the contents are not watered down. Quit looking at the ceiling.

Index

About
the Author

hristine J. Lueders grew up in the suburbs of Chicago and started her career as a busser at the age of 16 and was quickly promoted to server. Over the past 30 years she has worked in every front of the house position - from truck stop cafes to fine dining - married, and raised two children. During her time as a waitress, she trained hundreds of other servers, and before long she found herself managing a family-owned restaurant with a staff of 40 employees. Since then, she has managed three upscale restaurants, trained multiple managers, and she has created three waitstaff training programs. She has also assisted in opening two family-owned restaurants and one corporate restaurant. Throughout her career she also put herself through collage and received a B.A. in business administration with a concentration in hospitality from the University of New Hampshire. She recently moved back to Chicago to take care of her mom whom she missed over that long extended time away.